Breaking It Down and Connecting the Dots

Creating Common Ground Where Contention Rules

Peter Altschul

BREAKING IT DOWN AND CONNECTING THE DOTS
CREATING COMMON GROUND WHERE CONTENTION RULES

iUniverse books may be ordered through booksellers or by contacting:

iUniverse
1663 Liberty Drive
Bloomington, IN 47403
www.iuniverse.com
1-800-Authors (1-800-288-4677)

Because of the dynamic nature of the Internet, any web addresses or links contained in this book may have changed since publication and may no longer be valid. The views expressed in this work are solely those of the author and do not necessarily reflect the views of the publisher, and the publisher hereby disclaims any responsibility for them.

Scripture quotations marked KJV are from the Holy Bible, King James Version (Authorized Version). First published in 1611. Quoted from the KJV Classic Reference Bible, Copyright © 1983 by The Zondervan Corporation.

Scripture quotations marked NIV are taken from the Holy Bible, New International Version®. NIV®. Copyright © 1973, 1978, 1984 by International Bible Society. Used by permission of Zondervan. All rights reserved.

Scripture quotations marked NASB are taken from the New American Standard Bible®, Copyright © 1960, 1962, 1963, 1968, 1971, 1972, 1973, 1975, 1977, 1995 by The Lockman Foundation.

Any people depicted in stock imagery provided by Thinkstock are models, and such images are being used for illustrative purposes only. Certain stock imagery © Thinkstock.

ISBN: 978-1-5320-3039-0 (sc)
ISBN: 978-1-5320-3040-6 (e)

Library of Congress Control Number: 2017913024

Print information available on the last page.

iUniverse rev. date: 09/08/2017

CONTENTS

Introduction ix

Acknowledgements xi

Part I – Influencing

Not Motivation, But 1

My Biggest Fan 4

Video Game Parenting 6

In Praise of Equality 8

Kicked by a Camel, Kissed by Two Dolphins 11

Lab Assistant 14

Fifteen Years Ago 16

Jules Labrador 19

A Blizzard of Rewards 21

Cool Paw Luke 23

Part II – Workplace Behavior

The Disability Test 29

Two Truths and a Lie 32

The Grunnings Organization 35

Remembering Michael 37

Scars 40

Diversity's Bottom Line 42

Practice! 44

Leadership Is for Everyone 47

Disability and the Evolving Workplace 49

Part III – Intersectionality

Intersectionality 53

What If He Had Been Black? 56

The Gay Choice 58

First, the Gays. Then 61

Believe It Or Not 64

We Will Get By 66

Pioneering Perils 68

Universal Design 71

Disability and Diversity 73

Part IV – On the Couch

An Impostor at Busch 77

Fan, Not Fanatic 79

Sportscaster Bias 81

Let Justice Roll 83

Rock Bridge High 86

The Football Player 88

The Cam-era Effect 90

Kissing Grandma 92

Sound Power 94

Remember the Name 96

Porn Shades 98

The Greatest 100

Part V – Rhetorical Rabbit Holes

The Elephant and Its Rider 105

A Conversation with Mayor Koch 107

Role Reversal 110

Rays of Light 112

Two Controversy Tales 114

Bombast Matters 117

Trash Talk..119
Dear American Conservative Christians.............................122
Our Better Angels...125

Part VI – Music

One Of Those 129
It Was Fifty Years Ago...131
Fascinating Meters 133
Banging the Drum Loudly...135
Requiem Remembrances 137
Remembering Janiece..139
Tea...141
The Vibrant Poets Society 143
Mystery of the Dead...146
Hooked on Marty...149
Cheesy Corn...151
Yacht Rock..153

Part VII – Culture War

Love Is Blind..159
Good Enough 162
A Bias Towards Speed 164
Rand Paul's Smokescreen 167
Invasion of the Red Herring...170
Trade Trials...172
Smallball Health Care..174

Part VIII – POTUS Politics

Feelings Trump Thoughts 179
Dog Days...181
Donald Trumps Rush 184
Trailblazing Trials 186

Size Matters 188

The Shaggy Dog Partnership.. 190

POTUS for an Hour..193

New Swamp Creature Discovered 196

An Eerie Symmetry...198

Another Armchair Diagnosis.. 200

Pence for President! 202

Part IX – Christians and Christianity

The Politics of God Is Love 207

Drive-By Evangelism..210

Into the Ditch 212

Forgiveness Courage..214

Let Freedom Ring 216

Jesus Through Harry...218

King with a Heart 220

The Antichrist Parlor Game... 222

Curtains and Muslins.. 225

Peace 228

INTRODUCTION

In 2012, my memoir, *Breaking Barriers: Working and Loving While Blind,* was published. My goal for that book was to tell a good story while reflecting on the human-dog bond, what distinguishes effective from ineffective organizations, the power of ceremony, and the challenges living in a world where people with disabilities are viewed either as all-powerful gods or pathetic pawns. The goal of this book is to convey my thoughts on a variety of topics while sometimes telling good stories.

This book contains a selection of blog posts I have written during the past five years on family life, organization behavior, rhetorical rabbit holes, music, public policy, sports, dogs, diversity, Christianity, President Trump, and a few other things. Each essay contains fewer than 750 words.

Many of these essays focus on lessons drawn from experiences interviewing for jobs, raising stepkids, playing music, training New York City taxi drivers, watching sports, shepherding dogs, finding common ground on abortion, leading diversity programs, and loving my wife. Others are based on my reactions to opinion pieces written by thought leaders from across the political spectrum. A few meander into snarky satire. Most suggest that common ground does exist if we can find the patience, skill, and grace to create it.

The book is divided into nine sections. I encourage you to focus first on those sections that interest you, remembering that if you don't like some of the content, each essay is short. Most of all, I hope you come away with the idea that we can work across boundaries to accomplish great things.

Peter Altschul, MS
July, 2017

ACKNOWLEDGEMENTS

First and foremost, thanks to National Braille Press (www.nbp.org). More specifically, its publication *Syndicated Columnists Weekly*, a compilation of columns written for large and small media outlets that NBP has put into braille and mailed to interested people who are blind. I have read this magazine for more than thirty years, and the quality writing it features has been invaluable.

Next, thanks to my wife, Lisa, as well as Ana, Joseph, and Louis, my stepkids, for being good listeners and patient critics.

Thanks also to those who manage AlterNet.org and Townhall.com, two sites that post quality columns from progressive and conservative columnists respectively.

Finally, thanks to all of you who have provided such invaluable in-person and virtual feedback during the past five years!

PART I

INFLUENCING

Where I write about how we influence each other through relationships (sometimes, with the help of animals), as well as describing several concepts and strategies that will make us better influencers.

NOT MOTIVATION, BUT

February 27, 2013

Two weeks ago, a social services agency asked me to prepare a fifteen-minute presentation on motivating staff as part of the interview process for a Training Specialist position. While reviewing the PowerPoint slides they had sent to assist in my preparation, an exchange with my sixteen-year-old stepson flashed through my mind.

"You can't make me do anything!" he said, challenge rippling through his voice.

"You're right; I can't," I said calmly.

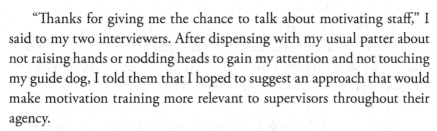

"Thanks for giving me the chance to talk about motivating staff," I said to my two interviewers. After dispensing with my usual patter about not raising hands or nodding heads to gain my attention and not touching my guide dog, I told them that I hoped to suggest an approach that would make motivation training more relevant to supervisors throughout their agency.

I next presented a typical definition of motivation:

A psychological process that causes the arousal, direction, and persistence of voluntary actions that are goal-directed.

I argued that while this was a fine definition for psychologists in academia, its textbook feel was less relevant for those supervising staff under increasingly challenging conditions. More importantly, social services staff understand that no one can motivate anyone to do anything, and will likely tune out if someone contradicts this belief.

After suggesting that there must be another way, I asked my interviewers what they felt while motivated. They mentioned being excited, energized, fearful, and focused. I asked what they did while motivated, and they mentioned being more committed to getting the job done.

Next, I asked them what they did to try to motivate" others.

"I try to figure out what makes someone tick?" one of my interviewers said hesitantly.

"Great; what else?"

"I try to do something that will resonate with the person I'm working with," the other interviewer said.

"Good; anything else?"

After a pause, I argued that motivation was not the best term that described figuring out how someone ticked and tailoring something to encourage someone to move in a given direction.

"You're not really motivating anyone," I suggested, "You're—"

Pause.

I tried again. "Not motivating, but—"

"In my opinion," I said when it was clear no one was going to guess, "we're not motivating; we're influencing."

I added that I had been trying to influence them to move in a given direction since the beginning of this presentation, and that I suspected they had been trying to influence me as well.

"Am I right?" I asked.

"Yes," one of the interviewers said with a smile in her voice.

"Influence is a skill that we can all get better at through practice and guidance while motivation is an academic concept that accurately assumes that you can't make anyone do anything. "Make sense?"

"Yes," they said in unison.

I listed some of the tools to influence people that had been included in the materials the agency had e-mailed me: money, perks, extra time off, enriched jobs, promotion, and recognition. I stressed the power of modeling desired behavior, especially when coupled with authority. I talked about the importance of setting measurable goals; encouraging responsibility and leadership; promoting teamwork; encouraging delegation, fun, and variety; and effective discipline. I concluded with the thought that feelings, not thoughts, drive action.

A dull version of the question-and-answer interview dance followed the presentation during which the interviewers told me that I would be contacted within two weeks to schedule a follow-up interview if they were interested.

On the way home, I reminded myself that while I cannot make my stepson do anything, I can, with patience, skill, and a little luck, influence him to head in a good direction.

And I didn't get the job.

MY BIGGEST FAN

July 21, 2012

"There's a plane high in the sky headed east towards France," my mom told me in a wistful, dreamy voice. She had come outside onto the deck of her house to join me on a breezy, humid Cape Cod late afternoon.

"It's certainly headed towards Europe," I responded as the soft rumble of the plane caught my ear.

"But I like to think it's headed towards France," Mom said in that same wistful tone.

Aunt Connie, my favorite aunt, had moved to France shortly after graduating from college. She was my biggest fan. Whenever she visited our house, she always said nice things about the music I was playing or creating. Aunt Sue, their older sister, would join them in singing trios and playing them on recorders, often fueled by French wines Aunt Connie had provided.

When I was seventeen, my mom, sister, and I, along with Aunt Sue and my grandmother, visited Aunt Connie and her family in Roscoff, France, a small fishing village near the English Channel. At 7 AM every morning, seagulls squawked my sister and me awake. Family members cheered me on as I explored several pipe organs in large cathedrals and small churches that were built in the seventeenth and eighteenth centuries, with Aunt Connie cheering the loudest. I rode on the backs of mopeds and tandem bicycles to sidewalk cafes to drink wine and eat crepes. I swam in an icy salt-water pool and chowed down on fresh seafood, artichokes, and pastries, surrounded by exuberant conversations that switched seamlessly between French and English.

Nearly twenty-five years later, I again visited Aunt Connie in Roscoff, this time with Lisa, my future wife. We settled into a drafty room at her rambling, vibrant house. In the mornings, we feasted on homegrown strawberries and fresh pastries, and devoured crepes, seafood, and fresh vegetables, washing it down with local wines and hard ciders during the afternoons and evenings. Lisa's voice bubbled with excitement and awe as she marveled at the fishing boats, the Brittany Renaissance architecture, the ancient churches, and quaint shops we walked by as cars and mopeds zoomed around us on the cobblestone streets and gulls squawked overhead.

A large crowd of family and local dignitaries came to celebrate Aunt Connie's eightieth birthday. Lisa had agreed to play the role of the birthday girl in a skit honoring Connie's quirks, which was performed in front of tables littered with empty wine bottles and the carcasses of lobsters, crabs, and shellfish. After her bravura performance, Lisa worked the room absorbing congratulatory hugs and kisses.

"Absolutely charmante," proclaimed Aunt Connie after she stopped laughing.

Aunt Connie died in December, 2012.

"You're right," I told Mom on that Cape Cod deck as the eastbound plane rumbled out of earshot. "I hope it is headed to France."

VIDEO GAME PARENTING

June 18, 2016

Explosions. Rapid machine gun fire. Weird noises suggesting alien invasions. Bucolic barnyard sounds. Large sports stadium crowd noise, including play-by-play calls. Loud, foreboding music and edgy, erie music. These and other video game sounds wafted through the house as I did kitchen and laundry duty; wrote a book; composed and recorded music; looked after my guide dog and a pack of bouncy standard poodles; did some consulting work; and hung out with Lisa while staying clear of Monty, our pet python.

Communicating with my two stepsons over the racket could be challenging. It was sometimes hard to get them to go to bed or do their homework or come to the dinner table. Or even get their attention at all.

Being totally blind, it was hard to talk with my stepsons about the games they were playing because of all the visuals. But over time, I learned something about guns, military strategy, and zombie culture while discussing sports-related strategies. My snarky comments about the music resulted in conversations about classical music and World War II-era American songs.

My most successful parental intervention took place one night while my older stepson and a friend were playing some sort of competitive shoot-'em-up game. They were both in eighth grade, and, like me at that age, engaged in increasingly loud and vulgar trash talk. In the past, I had allowed this chatter to wash over me, but, for whatever reason, I'd had enough.

"Suck my cock!" my stepson bellowed.

"Can I watch?" I called from the bedroom.

His friend howled with laughter and told me I was cool.

And the trash talk ended within the walls of our house.

Not just for that night, but, as far as I can remember, forever.

I'm sure my stepson, who now plays college football, trash-talks with the best of them, but while he sometimes curses around us when he's frustrated or angry, he doesn't trash talk in our presence.

I suspect that my three-word intervention was effective because, prior to that time, I kept my cursing to a minimum, had a great relationship with my stepson's mom, and had a good-enough relationship with both boys.

A few months later, my stepson spent what seemed like several minutes attributing his loss in another video game skirmish to poor lighting.

"Get a dog!" I called from the bedroom.

"Did he just tell you to get a dog?" his friend asked, trying hard not to laugh.

"Yes," my stepson said sheepishly.

And those lame excuses were extinguished.

Being a stepdad requires navigation through and around emotional mine fields without those noisy video game weapons. But I do know that modeling effective behavior most of the time, having a quality relationship with their mother, a good-enough relationship with the stepkids, and humor can be effective weapons.

Certainly more effective than the all-too-commonly used weapon of rat-at-tat preaching.

IN PRAISE OF EQUALITY

July 4, 2012

A couple of years ago, my family and I spent the fourth of July weekend at a time-share near Branson, Missouri. On the way there, we stopped at Lamberts, a restaurant featuring rolls that servers throw at customers and large amounts of greasy Southern food. While waiting for our order, Louis, my then fourteen-year-old stepson, announced that he was all for women being treated the same as men but—

Annoyed, I tuned out. I've heard variants of this phrase coming out of the mouths of Rush Limbaugh, Dr. James Dobson, and other men who seem to believe in women's rights ... for those women who agree with them.

"Rolls, anyone?" called a waiter, followed by excited "over heres" and the sound of rolls thudding into hands.

"Schools treat girls better than boys," Louis continued, and he's probably right. Girls do outperform boys in school because they tend to be more compliant and organized.

"But why aren't there more girls taking science classes?" Lisa asked, a PhD candidate in biomedical engineering. She has a point; girls drop out of math and science courses as they get older.

"And if a girl hits me, is it OK for me to hit her back?" Louis demanded.

"Yes," Lisa declared. "You have a right to defend yourself."

(True, but boys tend to be stronger and heavier than girls.)

"There is a difference," I proclaimed in an effort to move the discussion to a new place "between treating people the same and treating people equally."

"What?" Louis asked. He seemed surprised.

I repeated my statement.

"I don't understand," he said.

Our food arrived, and the conversation drifted elsewhere as we began devouring meat loaf, pork steaks, fried shrimp, and burgers.

"Hey, what about this equality-same thing?" Lisa asked.

"Explain," ordered Joseph, my then fifteen-year-old stepson.

"You know about the discrimination blind people face while trying to find a job?" I asked.

Verbal head-nods.

I spoke about how many employers screen out applicants with visual impairments when they require that candidates have a valid driver's license.

"That's discrimination," Joseph half-shouted with a smile in his voice.

I smiled.

"This would make sense for candidates to be treated the same if the jobs required someone to drive regularly from place to place," I continued, "but more and more employers seem to be requiring this for all jobs."

"But maybe they want to be sure that employees have a way to get to work," suggested Ana, my then 22-year-old stepdaughter.

"Or maybe they're trying to screen out people with substance abuse problems," Lisa added.

"I don't know what an employer's intent is," I responded. "But many otherwise qualified visually-impaired people see the driver's license requirement and don't bother to apply. And I think that hiring managers subconsciously connect 'no driver's license' with 'cannot do the job.'"

"So there's more flexibility involved in treating people equally than treating people the same," Lisa suggested.

"And equality is sort of an ideal that we should work towards," Louis mused.

While driving home after a weekend of swimming, barbecuing, and boating, a statement that Josh McDowell, an evangelist and regular guest on Dr. Dobson's *Focus on the Family,* flashed across my mind.

Rules without relationship result in rebellion.

Rules maintain order and promote a treating-everyone-the-same ethos; we all must follow them or suffer the consequences. Respectful relationships change subtly over time based on the values and needs of the participants. They acknowledge the differences among us and work towards managing them in an equitable way. Quality relationships support rules, and dysfunctional relationships result in...well, the Brits sure know what happened beginning on July 4, 1776.

KICKED BY A CAMEL, KISSED BY TWO DOLPHINS

January 3, 2013

Two years ago, Lisa and I escaped to Jamaica for a week. On our third morning there, we decided to visit The Dolphin Lagoon, a recently-opened venue to commune with a camel and several dolphins.

"A camel?" we asked ourselves as our driver took us on a bumpy forty-five minute ride over the Jamaica mountains.

After checking in, we waded into the ocean, carefully stepping around slimy rocks and other sharp objects as Lisa described the fish floating around us. Afterward, we sprawled in chairs soaking in the sun and listening to the ripple of the waves.

"Hey mahn," a lagoon employee called to us. "Do you want to see our camel?"

"Absolutely! Thanks!" we shouted, jumping out of our chairs.

As we followed him away from the waves through a gate into a sandy enclosure, our guide explained that they were hoping to include camel rides as part of their services.

"He's as big as a horse!" Lisa gasped as we approached the camel. I sensed an unfriendly vibe, perhaps because in the past horses have chosen to bite me instead of the carrots I have held out to them.

"Is it OK for my husband to touch him?" Lisa asked.

"Yeah mahn," said the guide.

"Don't worry; he won't hurt you," Lisa coaxed, sensing my unease as we approached.

As I gingerly explored the scaly hide of the huge beast, I couldn't help flashing back to my mom uttering similar words while encouraging me to explore a live lobster when I was five years old. But the lobster bit me; my parents ate it for dinner.

"Let me get a picture," Lisa said, leaving me alone with my hand lightly touching the camel's side.

"Almost ready," she called as I sensed the camel move. Instinctively, I stepped away, feeling a slight shove in the ribs.

"What's wrong?" Lisa asked, hurrying towards me.

"The camel kicked me," I said, more surprised than hurt.

After assuring our guide that I was OK, we hurried away with threats directed at the camel in our wake.

As we approached the dolphin enclosure, we met up with another couple who would be joining us for our adventures there. After another guide explained briefly about what we might expect, we put on life jackets and headed towards mysterious clicks, squeaks, grunts, and splashes. The four of us oohed and ahhed as we approached the dolphins.

"Jump in," called the guide from the water.

We obeyed, treading water as each dolphin swam in front of us, leaving a powerful wake as they passed. Next, each of us ran our hands along the dolphins' slick rubbery "skin," reminding me of an unsinkable dolphin-shaped toy in my grandmother's swimming pool.

"OK mahn," called the guide, "who wants to be kissed?"

When no one volunteered, I agreed to go first. The guide led me several yards away from the others, and encouraged me to relax. It was a bit unnerving treading water with these powerful creatures splashing around me, but two dolphins eventually "kissed me," one on each cheek. It tickled; I laughed.

After everyone else got kissed, it was time to take a ride. Once again, no one volunteered, so I went first.

"Just hold on," coaxed the guide as a dolphin glided towards me.

"Where?" I asked as the dolphin cruised by.

As the guide assisted me in finding rather tenuous hand-holds, I thought about J.K. Rowling's description of Harry Potter's first harrowing ride on a hippogriff, a magical beast that was half-horse and half-eagle.

"Go!" shouted the guide.

I hung on for dear life as the dolphin surged around the lagoon. Everybody cheered; it was exhilarating.

After the others got their rides, we danced with the dolphins. We sang a Bob Marley tune to the accompaniment of high-pitched dolphin drones. Then it was time for the final activity; once again, I went first because no one else would.

"Just lie on your stomach with your arms outstretched," the guide told me as he again separated me from the rest of the group.

"What's going to happen?" I asked.

"Just relax, mahn."

I tried, and heard a rush of water from behind as a dolphin propelled me forward by my feet. Once again, everybody applauded; the dolphin's power was awe-inspiring.

As our driver took us back to our resort by a more scenic route by the ocean talking to us about his life and his love of reggae music, I thought about the ornery camel and the awesome power and intelligence of the dolphins. I thought about how this once-in-a-lifetime experience worked in large part because of the guide's ability to listen, to experiment, and willingness to work with a stranger who is totally blind. He hadn't taken part in disability awareness training, and had probably never met a blind person before, but his experience working with people and animals from a variety of backgrounds prepared him to work with someone who presented unique challenges.

LAB ASSISTANT

June 22, 2015

On a dreary December day in the early 1990s, my former brother-in-law came to my shoe-box sized apartment in New York City to repair a toilet seat.

"Go away, Nan," I heard him tell my eighty-pound chocolate Labrador guide dog, "I don't need a lab assistant."

Shortly afterwards, I started supporting groups, organizations, and coalitions to work towards changing something for the better with Nan, Dunbar, Gifford, Jules, and Heath acting as Lab assistants. These guide dogs, in addition to helping me get to meetings on time, played a small but important part in lowering the tension in the room.

During down times, participants would often comment on how well-behaved and calm my guide dogs were. They often would add some variants of:

"Your dog reminds me of my dog."

"I smiled when I noticed your dog shaking himself, turning around to find a more comfortable sleeping position, or grunting in his sleep."

"If your dog can handle the pressure, then I can, too."

Once in a while, my guide dogs would play a more active role.

During one strategic planning session in upstate New York, laughter rippled throughout the room while I was explaining an activity.

"What's going on?" I asked.

"Your dog just stole a roll out of a garbage can," someone told me.

"No!" I said firmly, striding over to Dunbar. "Down! Stay!"

Dunbar grunted.

Several years later, the pungent smell of onion wafted in my direction while leading a workshop for New York City taxi drivers.

"Excuse me," a participant bleated, interrupting my flow. "Your dog is trying to eat my sandwich."

"You're not supposed to eat in here," a cabbie growled at the sandwich-holder as others laughed.

"I'm sorry," I said a bit sheepishly, grabbing Dunbar's leash. "Come on; no!" I muttered, leading him away. "Down! Stay!"

Several years later, while running a workshop in Washington, DC for a large nonprofit organization, a loud, impatient bark interrupted the preparations of an afternoon activity.

"No!" I called over my shoulder. "Quiet! Down!"

"Woof!" he shouted back.

"Quiet!" I called more firmly as participants laughed.

"Woof! Woof!"

"Gifford wants to be part of the audience," someone said, over more laughter.

I unhooked Gifford from the table to which I had attached him and heeled him to where I was sitting. He lay quietly by my side, grunting occasionally as participants completed a highly successful workshop on managing diversity-related conflicts.

More recently, my current and previous guide dogs have slept near my stepkids to calm them down, and my current guide dog's presence helped stop a toddler's screaming during a wedding reception.

Kudos to dogs of all sizes who, when well-trained and loved, assist all sorts of people in funeral homes, hospitals, airports, offices, family homes, and other environments.

FIFTEEN YEARS AGO

September 12, 2016

At around 8:45 AM on September 11, 2001, I was on a plane taxiing towards a LaGuardia Airport runway. We were scheduled to leave New York at nine AM and arrive in Washington, DC about an hour later. Gifford, my guide dog, was lying between my feet.

At around 9:30, the plane raced back to the gate.

"What's going on?" I asked the man staffing the ticket counter.

"A small plane ran into one of the World Trade Center towers," he told me. "The airport will be closed until further notice."

An airport employee assisted Gifford and me to the taxi stand.

"Where do you want to go?" a cabdriver asked.

"Penn Station in Manhattan."

"I can't take you there."

"What do you mean?" the airport employee and I asked together.

"I can't take you there."

"What do you mean?" the airport assistor demanded.

"Don't worry," I said, my voice tinged with irritation. "He doesn't want to take my guide dog. This happens all the time."

"No! No!" the cabbie nearly shouted. "Nobody can go into Manhattan."

Not sure if I believed him, I asked if he could drop me off at a subway station.

"Subways aren't running either," another passenger told me.

I stood there, not knowing what was going on or what to do.

"Why don't you come with me?" the other passenger suggested. "My employer has paid for a limo to take me to my home in Mt. Kisco."

During the ninety-minute drive with the radio tuned to one of New York's all-news stations, I called friends in the area hoping to find a place to crash. Irene Cornell, a grizzled veteran reporter who I had heard since I was ten years old, interrupted my efforts when, in a terrified, dust-filled voice, she described the collapse of both World Trade Center towers; the ensuing pandemonium; and how she had just escaped.

The ringing of my cell phone snapped us from our horrified silence. The caller was Elaine, an old family friend, who agreed to host me for a night.

At around noon, I sat on my good Samaritan's porch as she went to pick up her daughter from the local high school. I thought back to my mom's description of how the Japanese attack on Pearl Harbor had ignited the United States' involvement in World War II, with all of its death, destruction, and sacrifice. I wondered if that's where we were headed.

I'm still wondering.

"Hi, Peter," Elaine's warm, musical voice called from her car's open window as she drove towards me. We hugged, not knowing quite what to say.

At her house, I tuned into Sean Hannity's radio show, and was pleasantly surprised with his stressing the importance of unity. Within five minutes, however, he started ranting about the glories of President Bush and the horrors of Vice-President Gore. Disgusted, I switched to a different station.

I haven't listened to Sean since.

The next morning, I boarded an Amtrak train one stop before New York City's Penn Station. I was vaguely surprised that Gifford and I seemed to have the car to ourselves.

During the forty-five minute layover at Penn Station, more and more people crammed onto the train. Every seat was full; every inch of aisle space was taken. The usual northeast corridor grumbling was absent; we all just wanted to go home.

Between Philadelphia and Wilmington, my seatmate eased into a story about how she and her husband had been staying at a hotel near the World Trade Center; how the hotel had been set on fire when the planes hit the towers; how they had to flee without much of their luggage; how they had gotten separated; how she had seen people jumping from the top floors of the Trade Center towers to escape the inferno while walking more than two miles to another hotel near Penn Station where she had reconnected with her husband.

As she told her story, my social work training kicked in. I realized that what this stranger needed was an empathic ear and a present mind, not everything-will-be-OK bromides.

"I'm glad I'm home," she said as the train pulled into a station near Baltimore. "I don't think we will ever visit New York City again."

"I don't blame you," I said. "Hang in there."

"I'm glad we're home," I told Gifford an hour later as we walked into the quiet studio apartment we shared.

JULES LABRADOR

April 6, 2014

In July, 2012, Jules retired from his duties as my fifth guide dog, and began living with a local family headed by Meg and Phil Darkow.

Two months ago, Meg called to tell me that Jules had become lethargic and was rapidly losing hair. He was ultimately diagnosed with Cushing's disease, caused by excess production of the hormone cortisol. Since his health was rapidly deteriorating and the treatment was costly and complicated, Lisa and I encouraged her to put him to sleep when she thought the time was right, and asked if she and Phil could bring him by one last time.

Meg and Phil carried Jules into our house the following Sunday afternoon and placed him in the middle of our living room as my new guide dog and our two standard poodles barked behind the closed door of our bedroom. I sat cross-legged beside him and tentatively ran my hand through his nearly hairless and bony body, dimly aware through my numb sadness of people conversing quietly around me. I don't remember him responding, but Lisa assures me that he wagged his tail.

Sometime later, she knelt beside him.

"Hi, Jules Labrador," she cooed.

Jules raised his head, wagged his tail several times, and sighed as she scratched his ears. His tail banged the floor several times when he spotted Luke, the standard poodle with whom he had learned to establish a live-and-let-live relationship.

When Meg and Phil rose to leave, I hugged Jules and whispered my good-byes to which he responded with what sounded like satisfied sighs.

We encouraged him to stand up, but Meg and Phil had to carry him to their van because he couldn't gain traction on our hardwood floors.

Thanks, Jules Labrador, for your workmanlike attitude and laid-back style. I will miss hearing you barking at the poodles in our house and in our back yard. I will miss the comments of strangers about your spots, which Meg's vet believes were an early symptom of Kushing's disease. I will miss your quirky and stubborn streak that caused a dog trainer to state that you were one part dog, one part human, and one part alien. I will miss your sighs as you squirm between my legs while I drummed on your hindquarters.

A BLIZZARD OF REWARDS

October 1, 2013

A National Public Radio (NPR) story (1) highlighting a good deed of a Dairy Queen manager grabbed my attention.

The manager, Joey Prusak, noticed a woman putting a twenty-dollar bill into her wallet that a blind man had accidentally dropped. When she refused Mr. Prusak's request to return the money, he refused to serve her and gave the blind customer twenty dollars from his own pocket.

Another customer reported the good deed to Dairy Queen by e-mail, which was forwarded to the owner of the store who posted it where everyone could see it. Another employee posted the good deed on Facebook, and the story went viral.

Rewards started swirling. Customers appeared from miles around to give Mr. Prusak money. Glenn Beck invited him on his radio show and offered to buy him a franchise. Warren Buffett, whose Berkshire Hathaway Inc. owns Dairy Queen, thanked him by phone for being such a good role model. The Wild, Minnesota's National Hockey League team, offered him a suite where he could watch a game with twenty close friends.

"The guy did a really nice thing," I said to Lisa after telling her the story. "I'm glad he got recognized, and that the media reported it; there's way too much bad news out there."

"I agree," Lisa said, swishing her brush through her hair.

"But," I confessed, "a couple of things disturb me."

"Like what?"

I talked about my fear that this incident taps into the blind-person-as-either-pathetic-or-amazing stereotype.

"But blind people are at a disadvantage," Lisa pointed out. "It's harder for us to know if money has fallen out of our wallets."

"True," I conceded, "but I can't help wondering if the same recognition would have happened if the bill-dropper hadn't been blind — or should that matter?"

"I don't know," she said slowly, spraying something on to herself. "But it's just the way things are."

I then told her about the dangers of giving too many rewards for a good deed, as one of the most thoroughly researched finding in social psychology is that the more an act is rewarded, the less interest the doer will tend to have in repeating it.

"But everyone's different," I continued. "Some are influenced more by money, vacations, and other things than others."

"It does seem a bit much," Lisa said, sitting on the bed, "but it's not the manager's fault that he got all this recognition."

"Of course not. But we want to see more of these good deeds, and this excessive rewarding probably doesn't help."

"I hope he enjoys his perks," she said, heading out the door for a visit with her friends.

We hugged briefly. "I agree."

"Because I worked for Dairy Queen when I was in school," she reminded me, "and it wasn't a fun experience."

Her comment triggered a third concern. The NPR story reported that a Dairy Queen spokesman had said that they were trying to figure out how to reward Mr. Prusak.

Research and common wisdom shows that, whether influencing guide dogs, kids, or employees, the closer the reward to the deed, the better. I think that the manager's quick action and Mr. Buffett's phone call were enough, but I hope the Merchant of Blizzards is better prepared to reward future good deeds of employees more quickly.

Thank you, Mr. Prusak; you've done good.

(1) http://www.npr.org/sections/thetwo-way/2013/09/20/224417791/praise-pours-in-for-dairy-queen-manager-who-helped-blind-man

COOL PAW LUKE

September 30, 2016

I first met Luke on a hot, still late June day in 2006 during my first visit to Columbia, Missouri.

"Hi, Peter," Lisa and her then fifteen-year-old daughter called as my guide dog Jules and I stepped out of the van in which we had ridden from the St. Louis airport.

Luke growled.

Lisa had told me about how Luke, then a four-year-old standard poodle, had sailed over a six-foot fence to terrorize cats and patrol the neighborhood.

"Hi Luke, you vicious dog," I called. He growled more loudly as Jules stood by my side gently wagging his tail. "And hi, guys."

During the balance of my stay, the dogs vied for dominance. Jules submitted — grudgingly. But they became allies when I moved to Columbia permanently several months later.

A year later, Lisa and I got married in our backyard. During the reception, Luke somehow escaped from our house.

"Luke just ate the musician's plate of food while he was singing," a cousin reported.

Wedding guests loved our back yard, the flowers, the furniture, the tent—

"Luke is peeing on all the rented plants," Lisa told me in a voice of amused horror.

People raved about the food—

"That horrible black dog just stole a cracker from a child's hand," Mom told us.

After the honeymoon, Lisa and I settled into marriage life raising three kids and engaging in a variety of activities. Luke maintained his independence, jumping over our six-foot backyard fence to patrol the neighborhood, often returning with snow, hale, burrs, twigs, and/or duck feathers in his fur. His insistent bark would wake me up in the middle of the night so that I could either let him outside or inside.

Luke played an increasingly important part in our family. He prevented several fights between my two stepsons, first by nipping one son on his butt and then barking or glaring at them when a fight seemed eminent. He sat statue-like in my path whenever he wanted me to pat him. He spent many hours on the bed with Lisa to comfort her during health-related painful episodes.

In 2012, Heath became my new guide dog. Shortly after we came home after ten days training at guide dog school, he barked his shrill I-want-something bark.

"Is he crazy?" Lisa asked. "He wants Luke's bone."

Heath barked again.

"What's Luke doing?" I asked.

"Ignoring him," Lisa said, laughing.

Heath never barked that way at Luke again.

A year ago, Lisa and I took Luke to the vet. He seemed to be slowing down: only jumping the fence two or three days a week instead of every day.

"He definitely has a heart problem," the vet told us. "If he becomes exercise intolerant, bring him back."

"Exercise intolerant?" Lisa and I laughed. "Luke will die suddenly from a heart attack in the middle of a strenuous activity."

About a week ago, Luke died of a sudden heart attack inside of our house at the top of a set of stairs. He was nearly fifteen years old.

Luke was cool. Always regal. Contemptuous of dog toys. Aware of his surroundings. The only dog who would consistently come when I called him — except when he was on neighborhood patrol. Incredibly loyal and empathic, especially when Lisa was in pain.

Everyone who has lived around dogs speaks of a spirit dog — a dog who bonds to them especially closely. Heidi, a weimaraner and my first guide dog, was my spirit dog. Luke was Lisa's.

RIP, Luke King Poodle.

Cool Paw Luke

PART II

WORKPLACE BEHAVIOR

Where I reflect upon how organizations can better recruit and leverage talent from diverse backgrounds to become more inclusive and productive.

THE DISABILITY TEST

December 15, 2015

I recently took part in a job interview for a middle management position at a large organization with a well-respected diversity program. I was professionally dressed. The interviewers were respectful. I answered their questions at least reasonably well, and asked questions that generated a spirited and friendly discussion. Fifteen seconds after leaving the office, I knew I wouldn't get the job.

After nearly twenty-five years' experience interviewing for middle-management positions at organizations of various sizes and sectors, I can predict with unerring accuracy after an interview whether the effort will land me a job. If an interviewer asks a question that is both disability - and job-related, I have a decent shot of being hired, but if not, forget it.

My most recent interviewers failed this test.

"But it's illegal for interviewers to ask such questions," people have exclaimed when I've talked about this test.

"Actually, it's perfectly legal," I have responded. "Under the Americans with Disabilities Act, interviewers cannot ask questions about someone's disability UNLESS the question is job-related.

"For example," I sometimes continue, "While interviewing for my first mid-management position, an interviewer explained that the job in question involved lots of travel, and asked about my experience traveling independently as a totally blind person using a guide dog. Other interviewers have asked how I `read` visual cues since a major part of these jobs involved leading workshops and meetings of people who are sighted.

Others have asked how I keep track of data and appointments since project management was a key responsibility."

"But people are too scared to ask such questions."

"Very true," I say. "And it's my responsibility to do what I can to put interviewers at ease. Sometimes, a response to one of their questions can trigger such a conversation, but the same response in another interview might fall flat."

"But your rule might not apply in every situation," some have argued.

"Absolutely," I respond. "It only applies if the applicant has a visible disability. When I walk into an interview next to a guide dog, everybody knows within three seconds that I am blind. But some legally blind people can 'pass' as sighted."

Colleagues have argued that I might have better luck if I disclosed my disability before I show up.

"Perhaps," I say. "I used to tell the person scheduling the interview I was blind. More often than not, the scheduler wouldn't tell the interviewer, and I sometimes got blamed for the scheduler's negligence. Even when the interviewer was aware of my blindness ahead of time, they were clueless about disability, which caught me off guard because I expected better.

"There are times," I sometimes continue, "when I do disclose my disability beforehand. I might have to request an accommodation because my speech software doesn't communicate well with an employer's on-line application form. Or I might mention my blindness if the job involves supporting people with disabilities. And, to some degree, this disclosure conundrum is irrelevant because anyone who googles me will learn about my disability.

"But ultimately," I always say, "when to bring up one's disability is something each of us has to decide for ourselves."

During more recent interviews, I have tried my version of the Hail Mary strategy if interviewers are perilously close to failing my disability test.

"Now that we've had the chance to learn about each other," I often ask, "do you have any further questions for me?"

While most interviewers respond with some version of "I don't think so," others ask "what do you mean?"

"Well," I say, "many people are curious about how I do key job tasks as a blind person, and I want to give you the chance to ask such questions."

"Good for you!" said the counselor who's assisting me to find a job as we discussed the interview over the phone. Her job is to partner with employers to increase career prospects for people with visual impairments. "How did the interviewers respond?"

"The usual. Something to the effect that they were confident I could do the job so they didn't need to know how I did things."

"That's ridiculous."

"It comes across as condescending," I said, in preacher mode. "If they are so confident in our abilities, why is the unemployment rate for blind people so high?"

TWO TRUTHS AND A LIE

May 27, 2013

Last Monday, I spent my final two hours at my job taking part in a training session designed to orient new employees to the company culture.

During the previous four days, I had learned about the major screens used to assist employees in answering questions from anxious people about government programs over the phone. Most of the screens contain fragments of information, meaning that I would need to cycle through from five to ten screens per call depending on the complexity of the questions asked, as compared to one or two screens during my prior customer service work. The software that allows me to hear what's on the screen required at least three keystrokes to switch from screen to screen as compared to one for my sighted peers, and the software designed to convert the information on the screen into braille worked only sporadically, occasionally disabling my speech software.

During the morning of my second day on the job, I wandered into the break room where two employees gave me an impromptu tour while continuing their conversation.

"There are two refrigerators and freezers," they told me as I ran my hand gently along the appliances. "But that ice machine hasn't worked for a while, and one of the freezers doesn't work very well."

"We also have three microwaves stacked on top of each other," my tour guides told me as I again gently ran my hand over them. "But one hasn't worked for a long time and another works only if you slam the door really hard."

While in the break room eating lunch two days later, a female employee quietly told a male supervisor that none of the microwaves worked.

"You can use the microwaves on the other floor," he snapped.

"But that means we'll have to stand in line to use one of the two microwaves there," she said, trying to remain calm. "And we only have a thirty-minute lunch."

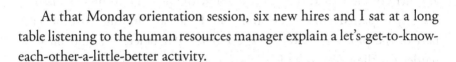

At that Monday orientation session, six new hires and I sat at a long table listening to the human resources manager explain a let's-get-to-know-each-other-a-little-better activity.

"Each of you must tell the rest of us two truths and a lie about yourself, and everybody will try to guess which of these three statements is false," she said, "and Peter, you'll be taking part in this activity," she called in a slightly raised voice.

"OK," I said, and when it was my turn, I told the group that I was a published author; that I was thirty-eight years old; and that I had been a human resources professional.

"I don't think you worked in HR," one of the new hires said.

"I did indeed work in HR for several years," I responded.

"You really did work in human resources," the HR manager said, her voice tinged with disbelief.

"I sure did," I responded.

"Wait a minute," another new hire declared after several seconds of awkward silence. "There's no way you're 38 years old."

"You're right," I said, assuming she had seen that most of my hair is gray.

As the HR manager began explaining the rules of the road, two prior interactions with her caromed through my consciousness. "Why don't you want to use the elevator?" she had demanded during my first day there after I had asked her for the location of the stairs that most other employees used. And her response to the issues related to the technology I was using had been along the lines of: "Don't worry, just trust us professionals" instead of: "Let's work together to see how your concerns might be addressed."

"...And you'll be assigned to a team when you get on the phones," the HR manager chirped, interrupting my thoughts.

"She doesn't believe that blind people can do HR work," I thought to myself. "Nor does she believe that blind people should be advocating for ourselves. How could she when she believes that we can't even safely use the stairs? So how can she truly believe that we can successfully do the work she has hired us to do?"

During my interview for the job on Valentine's Day, the HR manager and her colleague had complained about the poor performance of their visually-impaired employees, and now I had an inkling as to at least part of the problem: lowered expectations. If I failed, I would make it harder for the team to which I was assigned to compete; a fine way to make friends and influence people. Why bother making this effort while spending twenty percent of my salary towards commuting expenses for an organization whose leaders seem indifferent, if not hostile to, the needs of their employees?

It's been almost a week since I e-mailed my resignation letter, and I'm relieved that I no longer have to engage an environment that is toxic to me. I'm also angry at myself for taking this job primarily to placate well-meaning counselors who aren't ultimately responsible for the consequences of my decisions.

THE GRUNNINGS ORGANIZATION

June 23, 2013

Shortly after leaving my most recent job, I tweeted the following:

I just quit working for a Grunnings-like organization (#HarryPotter) that provides customer service; incompatible

In the Harry Potter series, Vernon Dursley, Harry Potter's abusive uncle, was the director of Grunnings, an organization that manufactured and sold drills.

We don't learn much about his managerial style. In the first book of the series, J.K. Rowling wrote that he enjoyed shouting at people, and in the second book, she described him coaching his wife and son concerning how they should treat a business client, taking time to bully his nephew.

Based on this scant evidence and the way he treats his nephew, Vernon Dursley comes across as a tyrannical micromanager with no tolerance for diversity. Most consultants would predict that his bullying behavior would force Grunnings out of business within five years; employee morale would be in the toilet, the good people would leave, and lousy customer service would drive business away.

But all Harry Potter fans know that Grunnings was in business throughout the seven books, or at least seventeen years. Moreover, the company was profitable enough so the Dursleys could live in a wealthy neighborhood, entertain lavishly, buy their son way too many expensive gifts, and send him to a prestigious boarding school. How could all of us consultants be so wrong?

We're not totally wrong. Bad bosses can contribute to bringing about bad behavior amongst those they lead. Those organizations with sound diversity practices outperform those that don't. Yet Grunnings-type organizations grind along quite successfully; how?

One of my mentors suggests that those assisting others to get better at what they do should identify key strengths that can be built upon when trying to change the way things get done.

So what might be the strengths of Grunnings and its director?

First, everyone knows why Grunnings is in business: drills, baby, drills. Often, a mission around which everyone can rally makes it easier for employees to adjust to managers with bullying tendencies. Secondly, perhaps Vernon Dursley's micromanaging tendency and talent at creating prisons from which Harry Potter couldn't escape without the assistance of a half-giant, a flying car, a hovering aunt-balloon, or an exploding fireplace also helped him work through the details of creating a product that was much better than his competitors. Finally, Vernon understood how to cultivate a client and close a sale, valuable skills that could be conveyed to Grunnings's salesmen. (I can't imagine him hiring any women.)

The Vernon Dursleys of the world can change. Towards the beginning of the last book in the series, Vernon grudgingly agreed to leave behind everything he knows to live with a wizard and a witch in order to hide himself and his family from the evil Lord Voldemort -- a major change given his hostility towards everything magical at the beginning of the series. I wonder how his leadership style changed as a result of this experience.

So perhaps a Grunnings-type organization providing quality customer service isn't so incompatible after all.

REMEMBERING MICHAEL

September 30, 2014

I first met Michael shortly after I started working at a wildly dysfunctional call center. It was my first full-time job, and he went out of his way to teach me about the arcane procedures we were supposed to follow while answering customer questions.

Over time, we became friends. During meals together and conversations by phone, I learned that Michael, like me, had been totally blind since birth. We were also recent college graduates interested in politics, music, and psychology.

Michael was raised in rural Connecticut by working-class parents, and spent much of his growing years at a boarding school for students who were blind. I was raised in a village about thirty miles north of New York City in upper middle-class surroundings, and spent all of my growing years as the only blind student in schools that I attended.

I also learned about Michael's frustrations with the organization at which we worked: how his supervisor regularly criticized him in front of others; how he had not been promoted even though all of us viewed him as the most competent person taking phone calls; and how he sometimes struggled to get out of bed.

As I began to deal with my callous and inept supervisors, he taught me about how to maneuver through office politics.

"You can't say that!" Michael groaned as he reviewed a report I had written detailing an example of management ineptness.

"Say what?" I asked.

"'Because of the incompetent stupidity of management'" he read.

"But it's true!"

"I know; but you can't say that."

"Fine," I said, annoyed and amused. "What should I say instead?"

"Just describe what management did and let people draw their own conclusions."

While Michael was eventually promoted, my disgust with the organization prompted me to accept a customer service job at a stodgy Wall Street bank, and when the bank outsourced my job to a call center in Jacksonville, Florida, I attended Columbia University's School of Social Work.

During this period, our friendship deepened. We compared notes about our challenges at work. He kept me centered whenever the liberal bias endemic in social work threatened to swallow me whole. We discussed music, family matters, history, foreign affairs, and challenges of living in a sighted world.

These conversations continued as I managed two federal grants and ran workshops for New York City taxi drivers while Michael continued to work at that dysfunctional federal agency. They continued, though less frequently, when I moved to Washington, DC to pursue professional opportunities there. We lost touch when I moved to Missouri to get married.

About ten days ago, I received an e-mail from a mutual friend informing me that Michael had died of cancer after a two-year struggle. I was shocked that he had died in his early sixties. I regretted not doing a better job of keeping in touch.

But mostly I'm angry. A regular theme of our conversations was Michael's commentary about how management sucked the souls out of the employees who worked with him. While he was eventually promoted to a position that best fit his strengths, he complained about spending several hours a day doing nothing.

"Why don't you try to find another job?" I would ask.

We both knew how hard it was for people with visual impairments to find jobs, and Michael, unlike me, didn't have other resources in reserve if his job search failed. The pension he had earned for working there for nearly forty years would have allowed him to lead a quiet life away from the racket of Brooklyn, New York.

"You just have a more restless soul than I do," he said during one of our phone calls.

I can't help wondering if the stress he experienced working with managers who acted more like dementors than people made him more susceptible to the cancer that killed him.

Thank you, Michael, for your listening ear and sound advice that I know you offered to all of your friends. Thanks for your ability to acknowledge the shortcomings of your beliefs and the strengths of the beliefs with which you disagreed. And while I wish you had found another job, I admire your willingness to stay in one place and make things a little better for those working around you.

Rest in peace, Michael Henderson.

SCARS

May 12, 2015

At the beginning of J.K. Rowling's *Harry Potter* series, Harry received a scar in the shape of a lightning bolt as a result of Lord Voldemort's failure to murder him. Throughout the series, he often knew what the Dark Lord was feeling, doing, or thinking through his scar even though they were hundreds of miles apart. This connection became a blessing and a curse.

As we go through life, each of us acquire psychic scars based on our experiences and our perceptions of how others have treated us. This is especially true if we are a member of an underrepresented group, as we are more likely to encounter prejudice and discrimination.

Most of my bosses have been from underrepresented groups, and as our relationship developed, each of them talked about their challenges gaining respect and promotions from their white male bosses and their colleagues.

I received a wide range of messages from each of these bosses's scars. I felt angry and a bit intimidated when one of my earlier bosses told me that she was entitled to discriminate against me because she had been discriminated against. I was embarrassed when a boss trashed her husband during our first meeting together, and bewildered when three other female bosses complained about the treatment they had received from male bosses at prior jobs during our second or third meetings. I was irritated when a boss interrupted a presentation I was making during our first meeting to tell me he was gay and to ask me what it was like working for the organization as a person who is totally blind. Over time, my colleagues and I grew to fear and mistrust these bosses because they were quick to blame us for their mistakes and slow to follow through on commitments.

I felt more relaxed and connected, however, with three other female bosses after they spoke of their less-than-positive experiences with their male colleagues in other organizations.

Why the difference?

In the Rowling series, Harry began to be able to control the scar-related connection with Lord Voldemort after witnessing the death of a house-elf who had helped him and his friends escape from danger. As he dug a grave for his house-elf friend, he found that he could close his mind against the anger the Dark Lord was experiencing. He was able to gain total control of his scar after allowing Lord Voldemort to try to kill him, and ultimately, by killing the Dark Lord in a duel.

Like Harry, the three bosses with whom I felt more connected after they shared their negative experiences with white males seemed to have more control of their scars. They talked of their experiences with less bitterness and more humor than their counterparts after first spending several months developing a relationship with me based on high expectations and shared responsibility. Most of my colleagues trusted and respected these bosses most of the time.

Fortunately, we don't need to go through near-death experiences to gain more control of our scars, nor do we need to forget about them. We do, however, need to start a journey that leads to forgiveness, or at least begin developing a different perspective about these experiences. Those who control their scars' messages become much more powerful leaders.

So what messages are our scars communicating to others? And what are we doing to influence the scars of people we encounter?

DIVERSITY'S BOTTOM LINE

March 1, 2017

Since at least 2010, the business press has highlighted research showing that diversity enhances creativity, opens new markets, and, generally, increases profits. But how strong is the connection between addressing biases and enhancing creativity? How well do other diversity best practices in areas of recruiting, onboarding, and training support organizations to leverage diversity's benefits?

Like most change efforts, unclear goals, poor planning, lack of leadership commitment, and unpredictable external forces cause diversity initiatives to go awry. Like other consultants who try to guide organizations through managing change, we diversity consultants can sidetrack well-meaning but ill-prepared leaders.

For diversity is not about focusing on bias or promoting cross-cultural communication or enhancing empathy. It's not even about overhauling the recruitment process, developing mentoring programs, and creating resource groups. These are methods, not goals.

The primary focus of diversity initiatives, I believe, is to sharpen organization skills at managing the inevitable conflicts that emerge when people of diverse backgrounds come together to work towards some agreed-upon goal.

Conflict can be a scary word, evoking images of shouting, sabotaging, fighting, killing, and other forms of nastiness. Yet, at bottom, conflict is merely something that is in opposition to something else. It's a part of life, something at which we all are pretty good at managing at times, and not so good at other times. Conflict can even be exhilarating.

In reviewing ten diversity-related articles I have saved during the past five years, I discovered that the word "conflict" appears only three times: twice in an article describing how some women make it more difficult for other women to succeed and once in an article describing how difficult it can be to correct biases. Yet diversity and conflict are inextricably linked.

Creativity, like diversity, is also conflict-driven: what boundaries to keep, what ideas to build on, how to create something new with these building blocks, and the quirks of those doing the creating. If we diversity thought leaders avoid the diversity-conflict link, we are encouraging those we lead to avoid it as well — to the detriment of everyone.

Viewing diversity through a conflict management lens still requires setting and enforcing clear behavioral boundaries, as sexual harassment, demeaning talk, and discriminatory behavior are conflicts that need to be managed effectively to prevent uglier conflicts from emerging. But this lens might encourage diversity trainers to start with a discussion about the inevitability of conflict and how it connects with diversity, followed by each participant sharing stories of how they successfully addressed a conflict with someone significantly different from them. This might lead to a discussion of successful strategies and participants role-playing diversity-related conflicts they are experiencing or observing in their organization.

Might educating people about biases each of us subconsciously carry be valuable? Probably, in the context of strengthening relationships so that conflicts can be addressed more effectively. Perhaps, sharpening skills connected with emotional intelligence instead of cultural awareness workshops or sensitivity training might be more effective in supporting people to manage those inevitable conflicts.

Other diversity best practices could benefit from this lens. Interviewers might ask prospective new hires to share examples of how they partnered with someone significantly different from themselves to accomplish something worthwhile. Mentors and members of resource groups might be recruited based in part on their ability to roll with conflict.

With diversity-related conflicts festering around us, it's time to reassemble the diversity building blocks — those best practices — using conflict as the foundation.

PRACTICE!

July 16, 2012

How many times have we left some sort of diversity training feeling bored, disconnected, and perhaps a bit guilty (but not motivated to do anything about the guilt)? How might we increase the possibility that these experiences might result in real change? I recently led a session where ten people with visual impairments wrestled with these questions.

I began by splitting participants into three groups and asked each group to come up with goals for a day-long diversity workshop. After several minutes, I asked each group to share their goals with the rest of us; they included:

* Educating about the business case for diversity and best practices;
* Exploring what diversity means; and
* Enhancing communication skills and the ability to respect others.

I next asked whether they believed diversity was more about increasing knowledge or developing skills. Contradictory responses bounced off the walls.

"Why skills?" I asked, handing a microphone to a woman so that people who were hard of hearing could follow the discussion better.

"You're trying to help people do things better," she said.

"But," protested a man from across the room.

"Hold on," I said, striding over and handing him the microphone.

"People need to be given information to understand better why diversity is important," he argued."

"But if I'm hearing you right," I said, "increasing knowledge is a method to motivate people to develop skills."

After some more give and take, I argued that diversity is far more about skill development than increasing knowledge.

"So how do you increase knowledge?" I asked. Participants suggested reading, asking questions, listening to lectures, and doing research.

"And how do you develop skills?"

"Practice!" a man half-shouted from the back of the room.

"That's right," I agreed. "And if you spend most of your time reading about something, you may be increasing your knowledge but not increasing your ability to do that thing better. And if you spend most of your time dispensing information instead of developing skills while doing diversity work, you're wasting everyone's time."

I then talked about how some organizations require up-and-coming managers to play leadership roles in nonprofit organizations both for PR purposes and to allow these leaders to practice working with people different from them. I talked about the reverse mentoring program I ran for a large multinational corporation where people of diverse backgrounds mentored members of their leadership team on diversity and culture change.

"But?" a woman asked hesitantly.

"Yes?" I handed her the microphone.

She talked about how an organization seemed to be dragging its feet after being ordered by the federal government to hire more people with disabilities, and wanted to know how to encourage the leadership team to start moving forward.

"That can be really hard," I said quietly. After some quick thinking, I pointed out that each of us have developed successful relationships with people different from us.

"What did you do to make these relationships work?" I asked.

The list the group developed included:

*   Finding things in common;
*   Being vulnerable;
*   Being yourself; and
*   Listening deeply.

"All of us want to be loved and respected," someone said.

I pointed out that activities like this tended to draw in participants because they are reminded that each of them already have a reservoir of strengths to draw upon.

"It's much easier to build on strengths than to start from scratch," I said, "and reminding people that they have things in common makes it more likely that they can effectively address the conflicts caused by their differences."

"And how do feelings play into this?" a woman asked as I prepared to wrap up.

"Feelings drive actions," I said. "Thoughts help, but feelings are the main motivators for change."

LEADERSHIP IS FOR EVERYONE

June 27, 2017

"Leadership isn't for everyone," asserts Tracy Byham (1). Before you take on a leadership assignment, she says, answer these ten questions that focus on your leadership-related skills and attitudes, and if you answer "no" to too many of these questions, don't lead.

But each of us engage in leadership activities all the time: influencing others to move in a given direction and/or supporting them to get there. We often lead without even thinking about what we're doing. Sometimes, we're successful; sometimes, we're not. But all of us lead others in big and small ways.

Our success depends on how well our skills and personalities mesh with those we are trying to lead and the environment in which our efforts are taking place. Anyone who has been a parent of more than one child will quietly acknowledge that one child was easier to influence and support than another. Trainers of guide dogs, after educating a string of dogs in the basics of leading blind people where we want to go, spend time thinking through which dog will work best with which handler, depending on how fast each likes to walk, how well their personalities mesh, and the extent to which a dog will fit into the environment of its handler.

Organizations constantly assess which employees who don't supervise others might make good leaders. Many managers promote the most effective employee in a given group into a leadership role, offering more money and other perks as a carrot. But this can be disastrous unless this promoted person can (or even wants to) lead others within the cultural constraints of the organization.

Stacy Byham's article is addressed to this best-in-group employee with a carrot being waved under her or his nose. "If you can honestly answer enough of my ten questions with a 'yes'", she suggests, "you'll make a good leader."

But these questions fail to take into account that each workplace culture can view the same behavior quite differently: compliant vs. assertive vs. aggressive; supportive vs. hostile; friendly vs. intrusive; and so forth. So perhaps a prospective new boss should consider questions like the following before agreeing to eat the carrot.

* What are my strengths as a leader? (good listener, clear communicator, good manager of conflict, other.)?
* In what environment do my leadership strengths shine most brightly? (one-on-One, small group/team, large group, other)?
* Describe how leadership takes place around you while you work? (rewarding/punishing success, punishing/rewarding failure, providing forthright feedback, clearly communicating goals, other)?
* To what extent would you feel comfortable engaging in those leadership behaviors that you observe where you work?
* How well do you think your leadership strengths will mesh into your workplace's culture?
* How comfortable are you exerting authority — that mystical, invisible force field that exponentially increases your influence by magnifying everything you do?

Leadership is for everyone, but constrained by how well our character and competence connect with the environment around us. We can widen these constraints with practice and support from others.

Often, the first step in growing our leadership skills is to become better at following others.

(1) http://www.ddiworld.com/blog/tmi/june-2017/10-questions-to-ask-before-becoming-a-leader

DISABILITY AND THE
EVOLVING WORKPLACE

November 7, 2016

October was National Disability Employment Awareness Month and Blindness Awareness Month.

Yawn.

Now, we're in November, and the unemployment rate for people with disabilities is still somewhere between 60 and 70 percent — or two to three times higher than our non-disabled peers.

Change is rippling across the workplace. Contract or gig work is replacing full-time jobs with benefits. Many middle managers are disappearing, with more work done away from the office. Employers are more committed to diversity due to demographic shifts and research showing how it can strengthen the bottom line. Technology is disrupting the way products and services are made and sold, with future job growth falling into two broad categories; high-tech: creating, debugging, protecting, selling, and servicing technology and its networks; and high-touch: assisting people to use this technology to meet their needs.

These changes can benefit jobseekers with disabilities. Working from home might assist managers and customers to focus on our skills instead of being emotionally disabled by our disabilities while saving us from the wear and tear of the daily commute. An increased focus on diversity's benefits might influence employers to adjust attitudes and be more flexible in providing adjustments to meet our needs.

But those of us assisting people with disabilities to find work must think and act in new ways. Sure, literacy skills, technological adeptness, mobility competence, and emotional intelligence are still important. But in this gig economy, we need to encourage a more entrepreneurial spirit, assisting potential workers to explore how best to use, build on, and sell their strengths in an increasingly fragmented and global marketplace.

Other challenges abound. During the past several years, technology platforms with names such as Yammer, Slack, Task Rabbit, MeetX, Virtualboardroom, Diligent, Boardpad, and Etsy have been created to support people to work together while apart, connect those seeking work with opportunities, and provide just-in-time training.

Which of these platforms has been most successful in the marketplace, and how accessible are they to the technology that we currently use? Better yet, which of these products has followed the path of Apple by embedding accessibility into their design? How can we best encourage those who create these platforms to be more user-friendly to those with disabilities while benefitting their other customers? Let's encourage those who work with us by buying and promoting their products!

Let's also explore how other coalitions are preparing people from other underrepresented groups to compete in this new environment. Let's form alliances with businesses to prepare people with disabilities to meet their needs. Let's work with officials from federal, state, and local governments to tailor Social Security, Medicare, Medicaid, and other programs to this new world, working with others when appropriate. Let's think about a basic income for everyone and portable healthcare, ideas with some support among conservative and progressive policy wonks.

Next October, we will again be bombarded with activities related to National Disability Employment Awareness Month and Blindness Awareness Month. Instead of yawning, how might we use this platform to communicate our dreams, goals, and accomplishments related to the rapidly-evolving workplace?

Let's get to work!

PART III

INTERSECTIONALITY

Where I explore the connections between people with disabilities and other underrepresented groups, as well as suggesting ways to benefit from these connections.

INTERSECTIONALITY

March 30, 2016

"Intersectionality," Google told me through the voice of my speech synthesizer, "is a concept often used in critical theories to describe the ways in which oppressive institutions (racism, sexism, homophobia, transphobia, ableism, xenophobia, classism, etc.) are interconnected and cannot be examined separately from one another."

Huh?

In a September 24, 2015 article in *The Washington Post* (1), Kimberlé Crenshaw, the term's creator, stated that intersectionality was her attempt to stress the multiple ways that the various isms were experienced so that these interconnected problems could be better understood and discussed.

"So," I thought, "a white guy who doesn't speak academese is doubly disadvantaged in diversity discussions. He is less likely to experience discrimination, and academic gobbledygook makes him feel unwelcomed.

"If I'm right," I thought, "then Mr. White Guy might connect with diversity better if its supporters drop the academic jargon, or welcome him into the land where academese is the primary language." After all, if intersectionality assumes that it's harder for people who are a part of two or more disadvantaged groups to break down barriers, then successfully addressing the concerns of one group might make it easier for members of other groups as well — if people work together across these ism boundaries.

Take, for example, police officers killing African Americans in ambiguous circumstances.

According to a report on disability and policing from the Ruderman Family Foundation (2), between one third and one-half of all those killed by police between 2013 and 2015 had a disability. Eric Garner, who police choked to death, had asthma and a heart condition. Law enforcement officials refused to give Sandra Bland her anti-epilepsy drug, which can lead to depression when suddenly withdrawn, and found her dead in her cell thirty-six hours later. Freddie Gray, a victim of childhood lead poisoning, died while in police custody.

What about employment?

We people with disabilities obsess about how and when to disclose our disability during the recruitment process, and how to incorporate it into our resumes. Employers encourage us to disclose as early as possible, but the unemployment rate for people with disabilities remains two to three times higher than those without disabilities.

I thought this problem existed only in the disability community until I learned about a study conducted by the National Bureau of Economic Research (3). According to this study, job applicants with white-sounding names needed to send about ten resumes before being interviewed, while those with African American-sounding names with similar qualifications needed to send around fifteen.

Some African Americans, in order to improve their chances, whiten their resumes. But, according to research conducted by Sonia Kang and others (4), blacks are less likely to whiten their resumes if an organization has a diversity statement on its website.

So did sending the non-whitened version of a resume help African American candidates when applying for jobs at diversity-friendly "organizations?

No, it made things worse.

Interests of the disability and African American communities seem to intersect concerning ambiguous law enforcement actions and workplace discrimination. What if members of each group came together to find those intersecting interests and develop strategies to address them? Coming together to express concerns of both communities will generate better results than if both communities work separately.

Perhaps, we could work with police departments to hire people with skills related to working across cultural boundaries while developing procedures to address concerns of both communities. Perhaps, we could encourage law enforcement agencies to do a better job addressing the physical and psychiatric disabilities within their ranks. Perhaps, we could encourage employers to assess candidate qualifications for jobs after names and addresses have been removed from resumes.

Intersections can either pull us apart or bring us together. The choice is ours to make.

(1) https://www.washingtonpost.com/news/in-theory/wp/2015/09/24/why-intersectionality-cant-wait/?utm_term=.0df8b5164b86

(2) http://www.rudermanfoundation.org/news-and-events/ruderman-white-paper

(3) http://www.nber.org/digest/sep03/w9873.html

(4) http://journals.sagepub.com/doi/abs/10.1177/0001839216639577

WHAT IF HE HAD BEEN BLACK?

May 31, 2014

During the past two weeks, Rachel Alexander (1), Walter E. Williams (2), and other columnists have criticized the concept of white privilege: the idea that European Americans still benefit today from the wrongs done to African Americans during the past 300 years.

Ms. Alexander argued that this concept is progressives' new censorship of free speech. She pointed out that most of us have had at least some indirect experience with blatant discrimination, and that these challenges can influence us to do better as adults. Mr. Williams listed a number of outlandish statements that were made during the most recent White Privilege Conference: "White people did not exist on planet Earth until 1681"; "The longer you are in the Tea Party the more racist you become"; and "Parents put their kids in private schools because they're racist."

I first became aware of the concept of white privilege in 1990 while interning at a New York City elementary school. While there, my guide dog and I attended a presentation by an African American educator who preached to us about slavery, Jim Crowe, and other horrors that African Americans had experienced, as well as how white people continue to benefit from these wrongs. His presentation irritated me, as I knew much of the information already, and I was struggling to break down my own barriers that were making it difficult for me to work with students, parents, and staff.

Since then, I have observed several examples of white privilege in action.

In the early 1990s in Portsmouth, New Hampshire, my guide dog and I went to a restaurant with a retired NFL player who was black. My guide dog and I had been served at this restaurant before, but this time, after waiting for twenty minutes, the waitress told my companion that they were no longer serving food. As we were leaving, my colleague told me that he saw other white people being seated.

In the mid-1990s in Binghamton, New York, I was part of a group of ten visually-impaired people and three sighted people. Before heading home, we stopped at a Denny's for breakfast. The table at which I sat consisted of white people, and the rest of our group — mostly people of color — were seated at a table near us. After I finished eating, I asked if the other table had finished their breakfasts.

"They haven't even ordered yet," someone told me.

They got served only after we at the white table complained loudly, and all we got from the manager was a hollow apology.

In the late 1990s, my then girlfriend, who lived in San Antonio, Texas, told me about how her thirteen-year-old son, who is white, was having trouble controlling his anger while at school, and how a guidance counselor had told him to be grateful that he wasn't black. My girlfriend's son eventually graduated from high school, served in the military, and is currently married with children.

But what if he HAD been black?

As a person who is totally blind, I can viscerally identify with some of the experiences of African American people. I too have been told that I couldn't eat at a restaurant or ride in a taxi because of my guide dog. I too have been mistreated at work because of my difference.

I also identify with Rachel Alexander's point that most of us have at least indirectly faced discrimination. My dad was raised in Dusseldorf, Germany in the 1920s and 1930s. Despite his family's close ties to the Lutheran Church, the Nazis declared them Jewish. They fled in 1936, and my dad eventually arrived in Boston where he received his PhD in chemistry at the age of twenty-two from Harvard University.

But what if my dad had been black?

(1) http://townhall.com/columnists/rachelalexander/2014/05/26/the-lefts-new-censorship-of-free-speech-check-your-privilege-n1843358
(2) http://townhall.com/columnists/walterewilliams/2014/05/28/white-privilege-n1843493

THE GAY CHOICE

March 15, 2015

I have always supported gay marriage since becoming aware of the concept in the early 1990s.

At that time, I regularly listened to Dr. James Dobson's conservative Christian program *Focus on the Family,* and my belief in the rights of gays to marry strengthened.

The Bible condemns those living the "gay lifestyle," Dr. Dobson and his guests intoned. All people who are gay can become happy heterosexuals, they argued. "And don't compare the experiences of gays with blacks," they harumphed.

Recently, Dr. Ben Carson supported these views by stating that many heterosexuals who go into prison leave prison as gay. Ben Shapiro (1) argued that homosexual behavior is a choice, while no one can choose to be black.

But Dr. Dobson and Mr. Shapiro don't define what they mean by "gay lifestyle" and "homosexual behavior." Might they be thinking about gay tendencies to like Broadway musicals and the ballet? Or their overrepresentation in the fashion industry? Or their sometimes distinctive visual and vocal quirks?

I doubt it, because these anti-gay marriage crusaders remain silent when their less politically correct colleagues trumpet their beliefs that homoSEX!!!UALS (they always accent the "sex" part) want to rape young boys and engage in anonymous sex. While a small number of homosexuals do engage in these demeaning and destructive behaviors, the lesbians and gays I know are caring, hardworking people who either want to be or are in committed relationships.

As to the prison-from-straight-to-gay pipeline argument, I have yet to see any independent studies buttressing Dr. Carson's statement that people in prison are more likely to engage in the "gay lifestyle" once released. Most people agree that most sex between prisoners qualifies as rape, and rape cuts across all sexual proclivities. So instead of implying that rape is a unique component of being gay, perhaps anti-gay activists could work with those trying to address the prison rape epidemic.

I do, however, agree with those who argue that the African American and gay experiences with discrimination are different, but what does it mean to live the "black lifestyle" or engage in "black behavior?" Or, for that matter, what does it mean to live the "blind lifestyle" or engage in "blind behavior?"

We all try to strike a balance between being unique and conforming to the white hetero non-disabled standard, especially those of us from underrepresented groups. Some African Americans straighten out their hair. Some work to modulate their voices to sound more white." A few jump from the liberal plantation to the conservative plantation where they bask in adulation while critiquing their fellow blacks' lifestyles and behaviors.

I'm grateful to my mother, who insisted that I stop rocking, poking my eyes, and other blindisms so I would be more acceptable to people who are light dependent. Unlike many other totally blind people, however, I choose not to wear dark glasses because of the physical discomfort I feel while wearing them, even though my eyes look weird to many in the sighted community.

So, Dr. Dobson and Mr. Shapiro: are my hard-working, caring colleagues who are lesbian and gay committed to monogamous relationships engaging in the "gay lifestyle" or in "homosexual behavior?" How does the "homosexual lifestyle" differ from the lifestyle of those heterosexuals who engage in anonymous sex or who rape children? And why shouldn't gays and lesbians be allowed to marry, as marriage discourages the sexual practices that most of us understand to be harmful?

Afterword

Lee Culpepper (2) recently argued that many men in the Muslim culture don't think they are gay when they engage in homosexual sex, believing instead that they only become gay until they love the men they're having sex with.

For at least the past thirty years, conservative Christian leaders have been peddling the idea that lesbian and gay folk either can't or won't love as well as we heteros.

That's why they lost the gay marriage battle.

(1) http://townhall.com/columnists/benshapiro/2015/03/11/is-being-gay-a-choice-n1968535
(2) http://townhall.com/columnists/leeculpepper/2016/06/21/what-do-you-know-about-homophobia-n2181181

FIRST, THE GAYS. THEN

April 6, 2015

In 1993, President Bill Clinton signed the Religious Freedom Restoration Act (RFRA) in order to protect people with sincerely-held religious beliefs from harassment from overzealous government bureaucrats. In 1997, the Supreme Court ruled that RFRA didn't apply to state and local governments, so state legislatures began passing their own versions of the law.

An avalanche of acrimony took place after Governor Pence recently signed Indiana's version of the RFRA into law, with supporters making the following arguments:

1. It's not really discrimination.

All of us discriminate all the time in areas ranging from what colors to wear to whom to marry. Disputes arise concerning what discrimination should be discouraged and what role the government should play.

2. Indiana's RFRA is virtually the same as its 1993 federal counterpart.

Judd Legum (1) highlights two differences between the two laws. First, while the federal version only applies to disputes between individuals or groups and a government, Indiana's version also applies to disputes between a person or entity and another person, business, or nonprofit organization. Secondly, the Indiana version protects religious practices no matter how irrelevant they are to core religious beliefs, wherez the federal version requires that these practices be central to a system of religious beliefs.

3. Other countries treat lesbians, gays, bisexuals, and transgendered people worse than we do.

Absolutely true. However, both Conservative Christians and gay activists remain largely silent on the plight of gay people in other countries except when sniping at those with whom they disagree. Conservative Christians also remain silent when parents living in North America who call themselves Christians throw their children out of the house after finding out that they're gay, or when coaches and teachers who consider themselves Christians shame students who come out in front of their peers. No wonder LGBTQ people are angry with Christians.

What other groups might Indiana's RFRA affect?

Perhaps those of us with disabilities who use specially-trained dogs to assist us?

We dog handlers with disabilities complain about Muslim taxi drivers who refuse to let us into their cabs because of their sincerely-held religious belief that our dogs, no matter how well-groomed, are unclean. This issue occasionally became a source of heated discussions during workshops I conducted aimed at improving customer service skills of New York City cabbies. The response from many Muslim cabdrivers was that the importance of doing good works trumped the unclean concerns — a view shared by every other Muslim I have spoken with about this issue.

Does the federal RFRA allow this form of discrimination? Probably not, because of the Americans with Disabilities Act and the fact that the RFRA only addresses the complaints of religious believers against the government.

What would happen, however, if, while in Indiana, a Muslim taxi driver refused to do business with me because of my guide dog? Would Indiana's legal beagles fight against this kind of discrimination?

Perhaps not, because taxi drivers with religious beliefs not central to

Islam's core tenets appear to be covered under Indiana's version of the RFRA.

Would those who support the right of businesses run by conservative Christians to discriminate against gays support those Muslim cabdrivers who discriminate against those of us with disabilities who use service dogs with equal zeal? If not, why not?

(1) https://thinkprogress.org/the-big-lie-the-media-tells-about-indianas-new-religious-freedom-law-539c35bb16f4#.v9nkjww6g

BELIEVE IT OR NOT

October 11, 2015

Once upon a time, a woman believed that her eyesight didn't mesh with who she was. After practicing being blind for a while, and with the assistance of a psychologist, several drops of drain cleaner were dribbled into each eye, causing her to become blind. Now, she's happy.

When my speech software babbled about this news on my Twitter feed, I mentally shrugged, winced, and vaguely wondered about the veracity of the story. Laura Hollis's (1) column posted on The Megaphone made this story more believable—

Until Norma Boge, a colleague who is also blind, pointed me to an article on Snopes.com questioning the accuracy of many of the details.

So much of the story probably isn't true.

However, the story raises a hornet's nest of issues, for there is a condition known as body integrity identity disorder (BIDD) that causes people to believe that something about their body doesn't belong. "How," asked Ms. Hollis in her column, "does BIDD differ from gender identity disorder (GID), which causes someone to believe that their body is that of the wrong gender?"

I believe that the two conditions are very similar.

Assuming, however, that drain-cleaner-in-the-eye story is largely true, it appears that the treatment that the woman wanting to be blind received was drastically different from the treatment that people with gender identity disorder go through: extensive counseling coupled with practicing living life as someone of the opposite gender prior to going through with the gender-change operation and follow-up treatment, all under the supervision of medical professionals.

By contrast, it appears that the woman with BIDD went through with the treatment in a psychologist's office after as few as two counseling sessions. She did practice being blind (called blind-swimming), but for how long, and under what conditions? How many people with visual impairments did she talk to while preparing for this change? Instead of dripping drops of drain cleaner into each eye, why not wear dark glasses, which many visually-impaired people do to shield others from their eyes' disfigurement? This is called treatment?

In her column, Ms. Hollis argued that people with BIDD and GID should learn to accept that their bodies are fine as they are, with the support of compassionate medical professionals, therapists, and friends.

But if BIDD and GID are similar, and many researchers believe that people with GID should go through with the gender-change treatment under certain circumstances, then why shouldn't people with BIDD be given the same chance under certain circumstances? After all, while a few of us are born blind, many more of us lose our eyesight through accidents or as we get older. And being blind, while sometimes irritating and frustrating, isn't the end of the universe.

Another question came to mind as I pondered this barely-believable bit of news:

Suppose that a treatment became available tomorrow that would guarantee that I could see. If I agreed to accept this treatment, would I be considered a person with Body Integrity Identity Disorder, and should I therefore be encouraged not to go through with this medical procedure? If not, why not?

(1) http://www.scoop.it/t/the-megaphone/p/4053125480/2015/10/08/laurawillful-blindness

WE WILL GET BY

August 30, 2016

The lyrics throughout this essay are excerpted from the Grateful Dead's song "Touch of Grey." (1)

Paint by number morning sky.

"Love that image," I thought in my urban bachelor days when I had little patience for the Dead. After moving to Columbia, Missouri to marry a Deadhead, I began hearing similar unusual phrases from adults and young people with learning or psychiatric disabilities.

Light a candle, curse the glare.

Many of these adults and young people don't like the glare of their surroundings. They seem intuitively to understand the phoniness encircling them, but find it much harder to play the game than the rest of us. "Just leave me alone and let me be creative," they sometimes nearly shout.

To try to keep a little grace.

Many of us, even with the best intentions, find it hard to connect with these intuitively creative people. They often feel out of place at school, in faith communities, or within teams that cooperate to win games or perform for an audience. They just don't have as many chances to experience grace.

To try to give a little love.

Since returning from the Grateful Dead's final concerts in Chicago, I have wondered how many of the band members might have been diagnosed with a disability if they were fifty years younger. One was diagnosed with dyslexia, and many of the others had trouble fitting in at school. But they spread a lot of love through the music they play and the lives they lead.

Like most Deadheads, my wife, Lisa, and her friends were (and are) extremely smart, quirky people that didn't care for the norm, and might or might not have a disability. In order to attend Dead concerts, usually in outdoor venues, they had to navigate long and winding roads, and survive heat, cold, drenching rains, as well as sometimes freaky drug trips.

There's really nothing much to it.

Over time, Lisa, her friends, and other Deadheads got better at working through these challenges. They learned how best to support each other during the good and bad times. They learned how to share supplies and be grateful for what they had. Despite the occasional drug overdoses around them, most left these concerts with the sense that because they had been surrounded with so much kindness, they could get by.

The Grateful Dead music and presence played a pivotal role in supporting Deadheads to get to a better place. Their lyrics are far more thought-provoking than your average Top Forty tune, and most of their music is quirky, transparent, and exudes a vibe of cheerful hopefulness. The major exception is the drums and space segment, but every Deadhead, even in a negative mindset, knows that this section won't take place until midway through the second half, and will lead to something wonderfully uplifting after taking their minds to new places.

"We're all misfits," the band seems to be saying, "but we'll get by. We will survive."

Most of Lisa's friends have done far more than just survive. One conducted research with apes in a remote location in New Guinea, and is now married to the head of the Peace Corps in an African country. One runs a successful business, while another is a graphic designer in Singapore.

As for Lisa, she spent ten years working as a registered nurse, has three bachelor's degrees, and is now close to completing her PhD in biomedical engineering — all while raising three kids, numerous standard poodles, and a python named Monty.

(1) Please click here

https://www.youtube.com/watch?v=wOaXTg3nAuY
to hear the studio version of "Touch of Grey."

PIONEERING PERILS

August 3, 2013

Recently, my wife and I had breakfast with Steve Kuusisto: author, scholar, university administrator, disability activist, incorrigible progressive, and all-around good guy. During the discussion, Steve and I discovered that we both have had less-than-positive interactions with a disability activist who parlayed successes into senior positions in two large organizations. I talked about how this person had called me at seven AM one morning to enlist my support in efforts to wring another costly accommodation from the organization where we both worked. When I said that I wasn't in a position to help, I was told that I was useless.

"You know," Steve fumed as we snorted ourselves into silence, "I'm tired of those successful disabled people who won't help others."

As our conversation veered in different directions, I thought to myself that Steve was right ... and that the person who we were criticizing, like me, has a significant physical disability and has spent most of her life as a pioneer.

I was the first person who was blind to be accepted at the small private school I attended through eighth grade and later at the local public high school. Since receiving my master's degree in social work, I have been either the only blind employee in every organization in which I have worked and/ or the first blind person the organization had ever hired.

Living the pioneer life has allowed me to explore territories that most other blind people haven't entered: playing percussion in my high school and college marching bands; conducting customer service workshops for New York City taxi drivers; encouraging pro-life and pro-choice activists to find common ground; playing a leadership role in launching the diversity initiative of a large multinational corporation; and improving the effectiveness of organizations assisting immigrants. I have had the chance to work with people with unique skills from diverse backgrounds. These experiences have sharpened my ability to communicate, manage conflicts, and solve problems.

Pioneering also has its darker, more lonely side. Making connections can be frustrating, as most light-dependent people have not been around people who are blind and have, for example, viewed my efforts to be friendly as asking for help. getting the work done can take more time and energy than my sighted peers, making it less likely that I will engage in chit-chat and get-togethers after work. Managers have often credited others with my ideas.

Then there's the sharpness phenomenon that a New York City taxi driver brought to my attention during one of the customer service workshops I was leading. He spoke of his need to be always sharp while driving in order to deal with dangerous drivers and unpredictable pedestrians; decide whether or not a particular passenger threatened bodily harm; and hustle to make a profit. Sharpness implies toughness, streetsmarts, an uneasy relationship with authority, and the ability to get the job done under pressure. These behaviors, however, can intimidate passengers, making communication more difficult and reducing the amount of tip money they receive while tarnishing their image with the public.

"The really good cabbies learn to balance sharpness with guarded friendliness towards passengers?" I asked.

"You got that right," a grizzled voice responded from somewhere in the back of the room.

Being a pioneer requires sharpness and a willingness to extend some trust towards authority figures, and while I'm pretty good at assessing situations on the fly and getting the job done, I have trouble trusting those in authority because, with notable exceptions, most seem both amazed with, and intimidated by, my skills and accomplishments. One boss, for example, told me at the end of my second interview that she admired the way I did good work independently, and that I might be a good role model for her father, who had recently become blind. A year later, she told me that I needed to improve my communication skills because I was more independent than her father.

So yes, those of us with disabilities and/or those who are part of other underrepresented groups who have achieved some success need to assist those behind us; at a minimum, we need to follow through on our commitments, temper our arrogance, and acknowledge those who have supported us along the way.

On the other hand, the tenacity, time, and energy we pioneers have used to explore new terrain often increase our sharpness while disconnecting us from experiences of others with similar challenges. Organizations committed to promoting diversity can assist pioneers by understanding our wariness of the system that still conveys doubts about our capabilities.

UNIVERSAL DESIGN

August 15, 2016

Universal design is one of those terms that gets thrown around when professionals with disabilities get together. Google the term and you'll find the following definition:

Broad-spectrum ideas meant to produce buildings, products and environments that are inherently accessible to older people, people without disabilities, and people with disabilities.

A corollary of this unwieldy definition is that products and services designed for disabled people can become valuable to others. People with strollers and shopping carts use wheelchair ramps. Medical professionals without disabilities use technology designed to assist disabled people to dictate text into a computer document to ... dictate text into a computer document.

I first became aware of this concept in the mid-1980s when Mom gave me a talking clock marketed exclusively to blind people. Two years later, my light-dependent aunt bought a similar clock at a large department store.

Over the years, I have found that universal design connects with sound workplace management practices.

While working for a wildly dysfunctional federal government agency during the 1980s, my visually-impaired colleagues and I complained about the quirks of our bosses.

"Don't worry," non-disabled peers cheerfully told us. "They're nasty to everyone."

While working at a large multinational corporation during the early 2000s, I began complaining to my colleagues about our boss.

"Don't worry, she treats everyone like shit," my non-Anglo, non-disabled colleagues told me, their voices dripping with contempt.

(I have also worked with several bosses who took my disability in stride, and most others agreed with me that they were terrific leaders.)

Organization bureaucracies often have a symbiotic (parasitic?) relationship with inept bosses. At that wildly dysfunctional federal agency, our bosses sniped at us; we ignored them. But we did share one thing in common: a contempt for the customers we were paid to serve. "All customers are liars," was a common refrain of my first boss, and most supervisors were ruder to customers than we were.

We visually-impaired employees sat together, and our neighbors would usually alert us to a new procedure in a garbled, confused way. When we approached our bosses, they complained that they were too busy to read us the memo describing the change. So we did things the old way until someone in authority got around to reading the appropriate memo. We quickly spotted the new procedure's flaws, which we discussed with each other just loud enough for others to hear while maliciously obeying every word of the new procedure.

Over time, we began noticing how others started using our arguments or following our examples. And over time, the performance of our office deteriorated.

Like people from other underrepresented groups, people with disabilities face unique challenges: less ability to control our visibility, an underappreciation of our skills, the tendency to be treated as the spokesperson of the underrepresented group(s) to which we belong, and the sense that we are often round pegs in square holes.

The concept of universal design suggests that products and services designed for disabled people become valuable to others. It also suggests that those inept bosses and the system that supports them makes everyone's life difficult, especially those from underrepresented groups. And those bosses who support those of us belonging to underrepresented groups to navigate systems that don't work well for us are generally better leaders for everyone, resulting in more productive workplaces.

DISABILITY AND DIVERSITY

May 29, 2017

In the 1990s, I began working concurrently on two assignments: managing a federal grant aimed at improving employment opportunities for college students with disabilities, and assisting in conducting week-long seminars to enhance team-building and conflict management skills. Over time, I learned that people from underrepresented groups share similar frustrations, and that strategies used to build relationships between white men and those from underrepresented groups worked equally well in forging connections between disabled and non-disabled people. Since then, I have been bothered by the separation of programs serving people with disabilities from those serving other underrepresented groups.

So I was pleasantly surprised when I read about the release of a new book entitled *Disability as Diversity in Higher Education: Policies and Practices to Enhance Student Success,* co-edited by Eunyoung Kim and Katherine C. Aquino and published in 2017 by Routledge. The book, however, has problems.

To start with, it is written in academese, the American English dialect that revels in ornate titles; places a preference on a plethora of polysyllabic verbiage; and contains a multiplicity of run-on sentences interrupted by lists of up to six references to research literature. Guaranteed to turn off most people not steeped in disability or diversity studies. I ended up skimming most of the book.

Like too many diversity consultants, the authors address problems using a social justice lens. Most people don't know what social justice means, and most to the right of Senator Bernie Sanders who are aware of the term view it as a politically correct weapon aimed at their character. We need some of these people to work with us.

Furthermore, most university employees, instead of advocating for "fairness in the distribution of wealth, opportunities, and privileges within a society" (a rough definition of social justice), spend their time supporting students to gain knowledge and skills to become successful. Isn't it more sensible to sell needed changes as something that will make employees more effective at what they're currently doing?

Widening the lens from social justice to organization effectiveness or systems change also allows practitioners to zoom in on a rich literature of best practices that support teams to move in a better direction. (hint: sensitivity training is usually not a best practice.) None of the authors in *Disability as Diversity* mention any of these best practices, except perhaps in the book's last chapter.

One of the more regularly-stated best practices for supporting change is to identify and build on strengths. So what are some of the strengths of those clueless, impersonal bureaucrats that seem to focus only on weaknesses of those different from them?

Respected professors who have learned to adjust to the quirks in each of their classes? Administrators who have developed programs popular with diverse audiences? Students and staff who somehow always make things better? Planned change efforts successfully under way that, with a little tweaking, can benefit people from underrepresented groups? A member or two from the leadership team who understands? How can we leverage these and other strengths to get us closer to where we want to go?

The problems addressed in *Disability as Diversity in Higher Education* are annoyingly real: people with disabilities being ignored, disrespected, pushed aside, admired for the wrong reasons, treated like children, and the like. The systemic problems — barely accessible or inaccessible spaces and technology, websites that hide programs aimed at disabled students, and hostility from members of other underrepresented groups — are also frustratingly real. But often, the best approach is to treat others in the way we want to be treated, hoping that others will return the favor. Sometimes, explaining how addressing our needs will benefit the entire organization will yield something positive.

That's what universal design is all about.

PART IV

ON THE COUCH

Where I consider how those activities I experience sitting or lying down connect with the real world.

AN IMPOSTOR AT BUSCH

November 1, 2013

Recently, my wife, Lisa, and I attended Game Five of the World Series between the Boston Red Sox and the St. Louis Cardinals. Lisa had scoured the web to find two seats in Busch Stadium's Champion Club at a ninety percent discount and a hotel room nearby at a very reasonable price. So we arrived two hours early wearing our Cardinals T-shirts.

But while I've grown to like the St. Louis team since moving to Missouri, my dad was a rabid Red Sox fan since fleeing from Germany in 1936. "You must root for the Red Sox and hate the Yankees," people advised him when he arrived, and my dad taught me well.

So I arrived in enemy territory not sure how best to show my true allegiance without irritating my wife and the rabid Cardinals fans. My first chance arrived when the waitress brought my first vodka, cranberry juice, and lime concoction to our table.

"Thanks for the Cape Codah," I said in my best Boston accent.

"What?" she asked.

"Thanks for the Cape Codah."

"Just ignore him," Lisa said. "He's from the East coast."

My second chance to show my true allegiance took place in the first inning while Lisa was away taking pictures of our surroundings. The Red Sox strung together two doubles to score a run, and someone clapped five times very slowly and clearly. I repeated the pattern.

"What are you doing?" Lisa asked sometime later when I again repeated the five-clap rhythm.

I told her that I was supporting the other Red Sox fan in the room.

"Just do it under the table," she snapped.

Meanwhile, we were taking full advantage of the free Italian food and open bar available to all fans in the club while listening to the radio play-by-play.

When the Cardinals came to bat in the bottom of the sixth, the score was one-one, and we migrated outside to sit with the real fans. But we could no longer hear the radio feed, so I had to guess what was going on based on the ebb and flow of crowd noise and Lisa's sketchy descriptions (she is legally, but not totally, blind). After the Cardinals were retired, I stood up to wish the Red Sox luck.

"What are you doing?" Lisa asked.

"Stretching," I said, trying to sound innocent.

We lost track of what was happening during the top of the seventh inning. I knew that something was going on based on the tension around us, and the occasional applause of two people far to my left.

"They'll pinch-hit for the pitcher," I declared when the PA announcer announced the name of the batter preceding him. "Something's going on and they can't afford to send up a pitcher who's rarely hit."

When the PA announcer indicated that the pitcher would indeed be hitting, I knew something good had happened, but not what.

"I think the Cardinals threw someone out at the plate," Lisa said when the inning-ending cheers wound down.

"Yes, but what's the score?"

We had to go back inside where Lisa could see from the bank of TVs that the Red Sox had scored two runs.

I haven't quite pieced together how those two runs were scored because we went to a postgame dance outside the stadium where we drank lousy beer and danced to hit tunes from the 1960s to 2013, all set to a house beat. On the way, Lisa introduced me to someone dressed in Red Sox regalia, and the two of us celebrated quietly so we wouldn't rouse the Red Bird faithful.

I'm thrilled that the Red Sox clinched the Series two nights later. I'm looking forward to the next season when the Cardinals might be unstoppable and the Yankees might get worse. What could be better?

FAN, NOT FANATIC

August 19, 2014

In 1965 and 1966, the Red Sox and Yankees were both terrible, so I happily chortled when the Yankees frequently lost and was happy when the Red Sox infrequently won.

On a late August evening in 1967, Dad came into my room as I was brushing my teeth.

"We must root for the Yankees," he announced.

"What?" I spluttered, nearly choking on a mouthful of toothpaste.

Dad explained that the Yankees were still terrible, but that the Red Sox were battling the Minnesota Twins, Chicago White Sox, and Detroit Tigers for first place in the American League. Back then, only the National League and American league teams with the best record made the post-season, playing each other in the World Series.

"It's still OK to hate the Yankees so long as they aren't playing anybody competing with the Red Sox for the pennant," my dad assured me. "But if they beat one of those competitors, that will help the Red Sox."

"OK," I said, somewhat doubtfully.

So I started rooting for the Yankees whenever they played someone competing with the Red Sox for the pennant. Miraculously, the Red Sox won on the last day of the season.

The following August, Dad took me to my first baseball game at Yankee stadium. Since the Yankees were playing the Tigers, who were once again battling the Red Sox for the pennant, we rooted for the home team — and the Yankees won! But the Tigers ended up winning the pennant.

Over the years, I have formed some strong opinions about how the world does and should work. But Dad's lesson that it's sometimes necessary, even noble, to root for your enemy to do well in order to support a good cause has helped me realize that people with whom I disagree make a good point or two, even if I sometimes have to take a deep breath to quell my irritation.

Most of the time, I'm a fan, not a fanatic. Fanatics root for their tribe even when it's clearly against their interests. They attack those in other tribes using words or weapons. They don't listen to reason. They insist on preaching at others instead of admitting that they might be part of the problem they want solved. They believe that all the facts are on their side, and that all the fanatics are in other tribes.

But all tribes have fanatics: Israelis, men, Arabs, women, progressives, pet-owners, conservatives, environmentalists, faith community members, business leaders, artists, educators, consultants, law enforcement officers — and especially fans of the New York Yankees and Kansas Jayhawks.

Currently, the Cardinals are playing the Red Sox. While the Red Sox are terrible this year, the Cardinals are competing for a play-off spot.

So I'm rooting for the Cardinals.

I'm sure Dad would understand.

SPORTSCASTER BIAS

October 16, 2012

Ten days ago, Lisa, my guide dog, and I were in our bedroom listening to the St. Louis Cardinals-Atlanta Braves wild-card baseball game on our SiriusXM radio. Late in the game, an Atlanta Braves player hit a pop-up that dropped between two fielders. Yet the batter was called out because of the infield fly rule.

The St. Louis Cardinals' announcers assured us that the right call had been made, arguing that the shortstop was prepared to catch the ball but backed off when the outfielder called him off. And under those circumstances, the infield fly rule applied, no matter where the ball was hit. They then described in great detail how Braves' fans were throwing bottles onto the field nearly hitting several Cardinal players, how the players had to flee into their dugout, and how it would take a while to clean up the mess.

"This is terrible!" they harumphed. "The game might have to be forfeited."

"I wonder what the Braves' announcers are saying," I mused, switching the channel.

"...terrible call," the Braves' announcers said, arguing that the ball wasn't in the infield, the shortstop was nowhere near the ball, and the left-field umpire made the call. During the five minutes I listened to their chatter, I only heard one brief mention of the activity going on in the stands or on the field during the delay.

I switched back to the Cardinal feed as the announcers were reading the section of the rule book about the infield fly rule which seemed to imply that as long as an infielder was prepared to catch the ball, the rule applied no matter where the ball was hit.

"...Bad call," the Braves announcers said after which they spent some time begging fans to stop what they were doing so the game wouldn't be forfeited — without describing what the fans were doing.

As the game resumed, I flashed back to my college days. I was listening to an epic Stanley Cup battle between the New York Rangers and New York Islanders when a huge fight between the players broke out.

"The Islander players clearly started this fight," Marv (yes! and it counts) Albert opined, and he and his sidekick described all the evil deeds of the Islander players.

"...The Ranger players are goons!" John (the Yankees win! — the Yankees wiiiiiin!!) Sterling shouted when I switched to the Islander feed.

"Absolutely!" shouted his sidekick, and they described in great detail how the Ranger players caused the fight.

Back then, witnessing how two broadcasters who I had grown to respect due to their fairness blaming the other team for the fight was mildly amusing, but now? Not so much. Like Marv Albert, John Sterling, and the St. Louis and Atlanta sportscasters' failure to acknowledge the complexity of what was going on around them, most of our national leaders refuse to acknowledge the shades of gray embedded in hot-button issues. Like the Atlanta Braves announcers, they either ignore or downplay the bad behavior of their supporters. And I am struck by how easily sportscasters (and all of us) can revert to I'm-right-you're-wrong thinking.

The evening after the Braves-Cardinals game, several of us were standing around drinking beer in a frigid, deserted parking lot after suffering through an uninspired performance by the Missouri Tigers' football team.

"That infield fly rule call was the stupidest thing I've ever seen," asserted one of the guys. "I'm a Cardinal fan, but—"

"The rulebook seems to say that as long as the infielder is ready to catch the ball—" I interrupted hesitantly.

"I don't care what the rulebook seems to say," interjected someone else. "It's called the infield fly rule for a reason. Besides, the infielder was nowhere near the ball."

So I now believe the umpire made the wrong call.

LET JUSTICE ROLL

October 19, 2015

Last Sunday morning, I woke up to the chatter on ESPN Radio about the turning point of the second playoff game between the New York Mets and Los Angeles Dodgers. The Dodgers' Chase Utley had broken the Mets' Ruben Tejada's leg while successfully preventing the completion of a double play, resulting in a four-run rally. The Dodgers won; Tejada was lost for the rest of the season; and I was blearily upset because I'm a Mets fan.

But I pride myself on being a fan, not a fanatic, so I spent the next several days trying to make sense of the chatter about the double-play preventing slide.

Was the slide dirty?

"Yes," most commentators agreed.

Was it legal?

"No," seemed to be the general consensus, with lots of chatter about not being near the base and rolling vs. normal slides.

But when the baseball powers announced that Mr. Utley would be chased away from baseball for two games, almost everyone — except for Mets fanatics — howled. Mr. Utley said he would appeal on the grounds that he had been sliding this way throughout his career without any prior consequences. Most sportscasters sympathised, arguing that while the slide might be dirty and illegal, players have been getting away with similar slides for more than a century.

Fast forward to the fifty-three minute seventh inning of Game Four of the Texas Rangers-Toronto Blue Jays play-off game, with more twists and turns than the 2016 Republican presidential campaign: thrown ball hitting bat, allowing Texas to break a tie; fanatics throwing stuff on the field; three consecutive Texas errors; a Toronto game-winning three-run home run; and more stuff being thrown on the field.

But the ESPN Radio chatterboxes have been strangely silent about one of the more disturbing parts of that inning.

Bases loaded with nobody out for Toronto, and the batter hit a ground ball to an infielder, who threw the ball to the catcher, who couldn't complete the double play because the runner slid into him. The Texas manager charged out of the dugout to argue that the batter should be called out because the slide was illegal.

"I think the manager has a point," said play-by-play broadcaster Dan Shulman as the stadium became eerily quiet. He went on to argue that the slide was similar to Chase Utley's slide.

"Or worse," said Dan's sidekick.

Eventually, the umpire upheld his ruling, and the noise level swelled as the game continued.

"Maybe it was the right decision," I said to Lisa as she monitored the cooking down of spaghetti sauce. "But I can't help but wonder if part of the umpire's decision was based on his fear of what would happen if he ruled against the home team."

While pondering the fairness of these decisions, I thought about how Chicago law enforcement had only made six drug arrests during the three-day weekend of Grateful Dead shows that Lisa and I had attended three months earlier. Really? With Deadheads known for rolling joints and consuming other illegal substances? To what extent did this low arrest rate have to do with the prosperous, well-behaved vibe of the Dead's fan base? Would the arrest rate be equally low if the audience were hip-hop fans?

And what does it mean when the Old Testament prophet Amos hopes that "justice rolls down like waters And righteousness like an ever-flowing stream?" (Amos, Chapter 5, Verse 24, New American Standard) How do we know that we're moving towards justice and righteousness?

I believe that baseball's leadership team should alert everyone that they will begin enforcing the no-rolling-slides rule during the 2016 spring training season — and then rigorously follow through. I believe that adults should be allowed to roll joints legally. I believe that justice has something to do with affirming life and promoting a level playing field.

Let's go Mets!

ROCK BRIDGE HIGH

December 5, 2013

Football invades our house in late August, with no firm retreat date. Joseph, my seventeen-year-old stepson, is the starting noseguard on the Rock Bridge High School football team, and Louis, my fifteen-year-old stepson, plays percussion in the Rock Bridge band. Normally, the season ends by Halloween — but not this year.

The Rock Bridge Bruins won their first three games handily, and were ranked second in the state of Missouri, but then lost their next game at home to an inferior team.

"They punched us in the mouth," Joseph told me after the game, "and we never recovered."

After defeating their archrival, the Bruins lost their final four games, the final one at home to a team that injured Rock Bridge's starting quarterback and an offensive lineman. The Bruins would have to play this team again on the road the following week in the first round of the play-offs.

No one was very optimistic during the first several days after the last loss, but as time passed, Joseph became more confident.

"We know we have the talent to beat them," he told me.

Then the father of Rock Bridge's starting quarterback sent an e-mail informing us that the fans of the team we would be playing were gloating about how their team had injured his son on purpose.

"We'll kick their asses!" Joseph stated as he left the house for the game.

Rock Bridge did kick their asses. And Joseph was a beast, according to several people who saw the game.

The Bruins advanced to the semifinals of the playoffs by winning two more games on the road. Several days prior to each game, the injured quarterback's dad would send an e-mail informing us of how the Rock Bridge team was being dissed, and exhorting us adults to tell our young men to keep winning.

I asked Joseph about his thoughts about the team Rock Bridge would be playing at home in the semifinals.

"They suck!" he grunted.

"So why are they undefeated?" I asked.

"They have a good running back and wide receiver," he growled. "But the rest of them suck."

The good running back ran for more than 300 yards; the good wide receiver accounted for 100 more yards; and Rock Bridge's quarterback threw six interceptions. But somehow, the Bruins won when that good running back fumbled the ball near the Rock Bridge goal line with less than a minute to play.

"A gift from God," Joseph told Lisa and me later that evening.

The championship game took place the day after Thanksgiving in the dome where the St. Louis Rams used to play. Around 100 people cheered the Rock Bridge players as they boarded the busses after eating breakfast at a local Cracker Barrel. (Louis and I got the attention of a local journalist by rattling a cowbell and hitting a wood block.) Despite our noise, the Bruins lost, but the team left the dome in high spirits.

Thank you, Rock Bridge Bruins football team, for taking us on a wild journey. Thanks for reminding us that the right combination of talent, good leadership, and the exhortations of an ornery dad can turn things around. Thanks, Joseph, for answering my questions and pretending to listen to my advice.

Rock Bridge high, Rock Bridge low; Rock Bridge rocks Wherever they go.

THE FOOTBALL PLAYER

March 23, 2017

Near the start of a ten-day training program about five years ago, Graham, a lead instructor, paired me with Heath. Young, powerfully built, and low to the ground, Heath had many of the characteristics of a promising football running back. Great vision. Exceptional quickness and agility. Outstanding acceleration and speed. Wonderful durability and strength. Good team player.

After the program, Heath and I remained in close contact, and while his football skills continued to develop, shortcomings emerged. His pass-catching ability, while never strong, got worse. Moreover, when he did catch the ball, he dashed all over the field, instead of running towards the other team's end zone. Furthermore, he often fumbled the ball when distracted or excited.

Like many football players, Heath has a strong affinity for food. For three years, Heath and his friends regularly raided refrigerators and counters, gorging themselves on anything they could find. This caused his body mass index to soar, ruining any chance for football fame and fortune.

Sad.

But perhaps not so sad, as Heath was born with a major disqualifying disability.

Heath is a dog.

More specifically, a black Lab who has channeled his football skills to become a wonderful service animal, swiftly swerving around people and objects as he guides me from place to place.

Recently, Heath was leading me through the labyrinthine passages in the University of Missouri's athletic complex while I was talking with a friend.

He veered in an unexpected direction, but I didn't pay much attention until my friend told me that we were just about to enter a locker room.

"For which sport?" I asked.

"Football," my friend said.

"Once a jock, always a jock," Graham quipped when I shared this story with him. Graham Buck is the Director of Training at Guiding Eyes for the Blind (1), the organization that trained Heath to be a guide dog, matched me with him, and nurtured the starting phase of our relationship.

Today, Heath attempted to greet more people than usual as my friend and I wound through the passages of the noisier-than-usual athletic complex.

"Why the excitement?" my friend asked.

"It's Mizzou Pro Day; the day that NFL scouts come to observe the skills of college football players throughout the state of Missouri," we were told.

Perhaps Heath was continuing his efforts to forge partnerships with a new cadre of scouts?

(1) http://www.guidingeyes.org/

The football player

THE CAM-ERA EFFECT

February 9, 2016

"Cam Newton acted like a real punk," a friend texted me shortly after the Super Bowl. "Wearing a hoodie and giving one-word answers to reporters, and then walking out."

I cringed, remembering the connection between the word "hoodie" and Trayvon Martin's death by wannabe cop.

"Haven't seen the interview," I texted back. "Reminds me of Trump."

Shortly afterward, I heard a replay of the interview, and Cam Newton did come across as distant and brusque. I couldn't help wondering, however, how my bratty twenty-something self would have reacted to intrusive questions after a public humiliation.

As I listened to the commentary surrounding this interview on ESPN Radio, I noticed how the increased number of African American voices was adding differing perspectives that were often absent during prior sports incidents that involved race. In October, 2014, several African American teammates had accused Russell Wilson, their quarterback, of not being black enough. The mostly-white sports talking heads, with varying degrees of vehemence, had accused Wilson's detractors as being petty, jealous, and/or lazy.

With the increased presence of African American talking heads, the discussion surrounding Cam Newton was less polarized and more thoughtful. Both black and white ESPN talking heads agreed that he had handled himself badly, especially as team leader.

But he had just experienced the worst loss of his football career; the interview environment was less than welcoming; and he might have walked out because he feared that he might lose control when he overheard a member of the Denver Broncos talking about how they had conquered the Panther offense.

"He must do better, and he will," several African American talking heads promised.

My friend called the next morning.

"Cam really did act badly," she told me.

"Of course he did," I said.

"But I guess he was under a lot of pressure," she mused.

I told her I agreed, summarizing what I had learned while listening to ESPN Radio.

"And he really does remind me of Donald Trump," I added.

"How?"

I told her that Mr. Trump had accused his opponents of cheating after losing to Senator Cruz in Iowa. "They're both sore losers," I concluded.

"I guess."

"And let's remember how trashing the media has been a major strategy that mostly white male Republican presidential candidates have used during their debates."

BOOYAH! to my friend for putting herself in Cam's shoes. BOOYAH! to ESPN management for hiring quality African Americans and giving them the space to shine. And a big Bronx cheer to politicians, business leaders, and others in authority who act like sore losers when things don't go their way.

KISSING GRANDMA

May 7, 2016

About a week ago, the Leicester City Foxes clinched Britain soccer's Premier League title, rising from the bottom of the league to champion in a year, defying 5000-to-1 odds.

Understandably, ESPN Radio's coverage of this rags-to-riches event was muted. While voicing dislike of soccer conveys an aura of contempt for the rest of the world, professional soccer has still not gained a true foothold in the United States sports scene.

However, the improbable success of Leicester City's soccer team received top billing last Tuesday on ESPN Radio's Russillo & Kanell show, when co-host Danny Kanell let loose with a semi-humorous tirade complaining that the Foxes clinched the championship after their closest competitor's last match ended in a tie.

"I hate ties!" harumphed Kanell.

"Why is it," I wondered, "that the part of the story that received the most coverage was the contempt for ties instead of the Foxes' improbable accomplishment? And why this contempt for ties?"

"Ties are like kissing your grandmother (or sister)," sportscasters groused during my high school and college years.

While that politically incorrect aphorism has been relegated to the bench, sports leagues have concocted convoluted schemes to break ties to quench our uniquely American insistence that there be winners and losers after each game. Extra innings and overtime have been a staple of baseball and basketball from as far back as I can remember, with football and hockey adding their tie-breaking schemes more recently.

But why this insistence on breaking ties, especially in sports where concussions and other serious injuries are a part of the action, and are more likely to occur at the end of games due to athlete fatigue? Allowing end-of-game ties to stand would help untie the who's-in-the-NFL-playoffs knot while forcing coaches to be more strategic, as winning is usually better than tying. Allowing ties in hockey and soccer would eliminate the shoot-out, which is contrary to the team spirit of the sport. College football's tie-breaking approach feels contrived, and sports fans and talking heads still complain about the unfairness of the pro football approach.

We all need to learn how to win and lose gracefully, but we also need to accept that often situations yield no clear winners and losers. Sometimes, almost everyone wins. Sometimes, almost everyone loses. Often, no clear winners and losers emerge after the fog of competition has lifted.

Sudden death and other tie-breaking strategies should continue to be used in the play-offs, where determining winners and losers is essential. Less use of these approaches during the regular season might increase the tension and mystique of post-season games.

So let's explore the ambiguous beauty of the tie.

And for those of us with grandmothers and sisters, let's kiss them more often.

SOUND POWER

February 9, 2014

While living my urban bachelor life in New York City and Washington, DC, I almost always listened to the Super Bowl on the radio with my guide dogs sprawled out on my twin bed or threadbare couch. Now that I'm married, I usually watch the game on TV with Lisa, her three children, and friends, with my guide dog either stretched out on our king-sized bed or joining our standard poodles in pestering us for attention or foraging for food. Following the game on TV has become more challenging because the sportscasters describe what's going on in Tweet-like bursts, allowing the picture to fill in the gaps, while their radio counterparts describe the action in Facebook-like detail.

But the Super Bowl is also about the commercials, and watching them is often more confusing than the game. Since the average soundscape consists of nothing but loud, glitzy music or bits of hit songs, I often have to ask someone what product or service is being sold.

"Who cares?" some commercial-producer might snort. "You're an old-school totally blind guy who's mourning the triumph of video over sound. A picture's worth a thousand words."

It's also true that my teenage stepkids, and friends — all light-dependent — express confusion and irritation with these commercials.

"What was that commercial trying to sell?" I ask, plunking a beer bottle on the table.

"Who the fuck cares?" one or both of my stepsons bellow, munching on chicken wings.

"I don't know; it doesn't matter," a local architect harumphs, popping the top of a beer.

"What a stupid commercial," Lisa says, crunching a cracker.

There are exceptions. We became suddenly silent during the Budweiser commercial, and occasionally, my stepsons audibly gasp about some visual effect. Even I paid attention when Bob Dylan growled about the mystique of the American automobile and when a sandwich with Taco Bell's name written on it was in fact made by Subway.

But the commercial that really hooked me took place close to halftime during last Sunday's game. I was wandering towards the kitchen when I heard a child's clear voice sing the first line of "America, the Beautiful." Mesmerized, I stood still absorbing the unaccompanied multilingual version of a uniquely American anthem.

"That was beautiful," I said. "What product was that for?"

"I don't know," Lisa called. "But it was beautiful."

I learned later that Coke paid for that commercial after reading about the firestorm it created when some conservatives complained that this uniquely American anthem wasn't sung just in English.

I get that the Super Bowl is about excess. We fans eat and drink too much junk food while watching huge, talented men display their skills, smarts, and teamwork. I understand that you commercial-makers are encouraged to show your overwhelming creativity and ability to use the latest technological gadgets. Yes, you're making your creations more for your colleagues than us viewers. But doesn't it bother you at least a little when some in your audience either don't know or care to know which products you are trying to sell?

I get that video has killed the radio star, and that pictures can be powerful props. I understand that talk and sound effects can get in the way of a beautiful tableau. But sound can be powerful, too.

So why not tell your story using mostly sound? Why not dial back some of the musical excesses? Why not create a catchy jingle during which the product name is prominently sung?

Creativity is about bucking some traditions while keeping others. Let's see sound and silence surface more soulfully.

REMEMBER THE NAME

December 30, 2016

Radio noise is always in the background as my guide dog and I hang out in a rather large, sparsely furnished apartment. 2016 has been a quiet, dark year with splashes of color borne through conversation, virtual gigs, music-making...and commercials.

Marketers understand that feelings, not thoughts, drive actions, and one tactic they use to connect with our feelings channel is humor. I often find myself smiling at these humor-driven ads, but I often have no idea of what's being sold.

One commercial, for example, featured two men preparing to parachute from a plane. It turns out that the student knows more than the instructor about the basics of simultaneous parachute-jumping, but the instructor says just before they jump, "I love parachutes, and I love people." And they jump together, their voices melding into a joyous, primal scream.

But the product being sold? No idea.

A more recent commercial featured a romantic tenor singing about being ripped off after carelessly shopping on the Internet to the tune of "Silent Night." This commercial made me smile, but I have no clue about the product being sold.

Then they're those commercials that market that insurance-selling organization with a name similar to that of a cockroach-consuming creature. Over the years, this organization has spawned many comical commercials that have inspired me to remember its name.

But how do you spell it?

Guycko?

Geicko?

Guyco?

Gyecko?

I have no idea.

Friends who are light-dependent have told me that TV ads for this organization contain graphics that flash the properly-spelled name. When I asked how the name was spelled, one said she wasn't sure, and the other answered in a voice full of uncertainty.

Then, there's Zyppah.

Through 2016, "Jimmy" has trumpeted the virtues of this product in a grating Godfatherly voice. Along the way, he has made snarky comments about politics, social media, family dynamics, and the self-help movement while promoting (and spelling) the name of this "snoring eliminator." This campaign has even featured two tackily charming jingles.

Ring out the old, ring in the new, but marketers might want to bear in mind that light-independent people with guide dogs are potential purchasers of auto and home insurance, cars, computers, household appliances, and other stuff. Marketers might want to consider hiring and supporting a more diverse group of creatives to help them connect their product better to the feelings and thought channels of potential buyers. And just remember that no one will buy what you're trying to sell if we can't remember its name.

Congratulations, Zyppah zealots, for keeping me awake and chuckling.

PORN SHADES

February 22, 2015

I look forward to reading my braille copy of *Playboy* every month. Ever since I started dating Lisa in 2005, I've read the "Playboy Advisor" to her while we're lying together in bed.

When people who are light-dependent hear about this, most first think I'm kidding. When I show them the image of the Playboy bunny on the cover, reactions range from amazement to nervous laughter to edgy silence. While living in Washington, DC, my boss, with a smile in her voice, told me that a picture of me reading a copy of Playboy with my guide dog lying under the seat on DC's subway system had made the style section of *The Washington Post*. The picture remained on the office bulletin board for days.

Last Valentine's Day, Lisa and I went to see *Fifty Shades of Grey*. Because we had read much of the book together, I could follow the movie through the dialogue, the audience's verbal reactions, and Lisa's whispered descriptions.

"The actor playing Christian Grey isn't as hot as I expected," she complained quietly towards the beginning.

"I changed my mind," she said later.

"The sex scenes are hot," Lisa murmured in my ear while describing in short bursts how ice cubes, hand-cuffs, feathers, whips, and other contraptions were being used.

We liked the film, which closely followed the book's trajectory. We were especially drawn to the sound track which used a diversity of styles to highlight the joyous, sad, sultry, and ominous shadings of the film.

Conservative critics predictably trashed the movie as another example of the descent of our culture to mindless depravity. They agreed with many progressives when they argued that it glorifies stalking and other abusive behavior, especially when done by someone who's obscenely rich.

Mark Davis (1) stated that the film encourages women to go along with sexual violence -- because maybe you can change him. He closed his column by stating that he looks forward to people trying to praise the *Fifty Shades* phenomenon.

I have no interest in praising this phenomenon, but as the title suggests, relationships contain, well, at least fifty shades of grey. Yes, Tycoon Christian Grey engaged in predatory behavior, but unlike most abusive people I have known, he was honest enough to say that he was "fifty shades of fucked up." Virginal Anastasia Steele had enough self-confidence not to sign Christian's bondage contract, to confront some of his hurtful behavior, and to leave when she could no longer tolerate the abuse.

Let's also remember that rough sex doesn't always equate with an abusive relationship. And I would take conservatives' critique of porn more seriously if they didn't reflexively praise films like *American Sniper,* where all Muslims in Iran and Afghanistan are terrorists to be mocked and killed.

I also found it interesting that, according to an article in *The Washington Post* (2), the top ten states for pre-release sales for the *Fifty Shades* film were Mississippi, Arkansas, West Virginia, Kentucky, Alabama, Louisiana, North Dakota, South Carolina, Iowa, and Tennessee. I can't help but wonder why pre-release sales of this sex-saturated love story are highest in states where conservative Christians rule.

As for me, I plan to continue to be available to my stepkids to talk about relationships of all sorts while trying to strengthen my relationship with Lisa.

And my most recent issue of *Playboy* has just arrived.

(1) http://townhall.com/columnists/markdavis/2015/02/13/50-shades-of-cultural-poison-n1956884
(2) https://www.washingtonpost.com/news/wonk/wp/2015/02/09/people-in-the-south-are-really-into-fifty-shades-of-grey/?utm_term=.0c054cebe91e

THE GREATEST

June 10, 2016

I never have been much of a boxing fan, preferring team sports. And I don't remember much about Cassius Clay's early boxing exploits.

While in elementary school, however, I vaguely recall my dad admiring Clay's prowess but not quite sure what to make of his pre-fight chatter. I also remember watching one of Mr. Clay's conquests on TV with Dad and a couple of other men; the fight didn't last long.

Then came the name change.

"Cassius" sounded strange, but the name "Mohammed Ali" (the way I saw it spelled back then) had an exotic, mysterious ring. Why would anyone want to change his name?

It got stranger.

This Negro Mohammed was a Moslem? What's that? Something to do with a strange religion called Islam which told him not to register for something called the draft to fight in some war in Vietnam?

The only thing that cut through my disinterested fog was my dad's dislike of this Clay-Ali character, especially confusing since I knew my parents opposed the Vietnam war and supported the work of Dr. Martin Luther King, Jr.

In sixth grade, four black kids joined the students at the small private school I was attending. This was my first exposure to black people my age, and while each had different personalities, over-all, I grew to admire and vaguely fear them. They called people out when they felt disrespected, even me despite my disability. They pushed me to respect the music of Aretha Franklin, the Temptations, Sly and the Family Stone, the Supremes, and

James Brown. They rejuvenated the school's pathetic basketball team. They were sharp, street-smart people who often didn't do their homework, which my mom didn't appreciate when I started not doing all of mine.

And they loved Muhammad Ali. They recited his poetry, far more ear-catching than the poets we were reading in class. They described in vivid detail his greatest victories. They occasionally tossed about garbled fragments of one of his more famous quotes about how he had no quarrel with the Viet Cong, as none of them ever called him a nigger or treated black people like dogs.

I don't remember who my father rooted for in the first Ali-Frazier fight, but I rooted for Ali.

I followed the rest of Mr. Ali's boxing career from a distance, becoming momentarily fascinated by his victory over George Foreman, courtesy of Norman Mailer's 1975 book *The Fight,* and saddened when age caught up with him in the ring.

Muhammad Ali was a talented trash-talker who backed up his taunts with action; a powerful, dangerous political force; an anti-establishment icon; and a devout Muslim who was generous, courteous, and courageous. Along with my African American classmates, he helped teach me how people living side by side with similar political views often view things quite differently. I now understand better how strong religious faith can influence people to take bold, courageous steps that might be otherwise impossible. I appreciate his journey from angry, black separatist to global humanitarian.

RIP, Mr. Ali. With Allah's help, you are the greatest.

PART V

RHETORICAL
RABBIT HOLES

Where I explore some of the rhetorical traps we set for each other that make it difficult to find common ground and suggest ways to avoid or overcome them.

THE ELEPHANT AND ITS RIDER

February 1, 2014

"Feelings, not thoughts, drive actions."

I heard this quote often from Kenneth Sole, PhD, a pioneer in the field of workplace diversity during his six-day seminars on managing conflict, addressing diversity, and exploring group dynamics.

Dr. Sole's aphorism recently reemerged from my subconscious while reading Dr. Jonathan Haidt's 2012 book *The Righteous Mind: Why Good People Are Divided by Politics and Religion*. In this book, the author argued that intuitions (largely feelings) drive our political beliefs, and that reason (thoughts) is intuition's servant. He painted a picture of intuition as an elephant with reason as its rider, and suggested that each of us can get better at riding our individual elephants.

So how can we support each other in developing our elephant-riding skills?

First, by snickering at ideologues of all stripes who argue that they, and only they, are rational. Sorry, dudes, but your elephant is threatening to trample you.

Secondly, by remaining calm when ideologues bellow statistics that support their opinion at those with whom they disagree, for even if the research behind the statistic is sound, the rider being confronted will find a way to refute it because their elephant feels ignored or abused.

Finally, by bearing in mind that the more enlightened ideologue understands that a good story connects with the other's elephant, and makes sure that only their story is heard.

These tactics might win an argument, but won't change the mind of another elephant rider.

In addition to making fun of the ideologues' failed strategies, I have found the following to be empowering.

* I remind myself that my goal is not to win the argument, but to state clearly what I believe and why.
* I try to listen more than I speak.
* I make an effort to find what connects me with the elephant-riders I come across.
* I remember that I am often wrong.
* I think about how finding common ground doesn't necessarily mean meeting in the middle.
* I try to connect on both the thoughts and feelings channels.
* I make an effort to end these difficult conversations on some point of common ground.

In short, the most effective way to influence elephants and their riders is to work towards creating supportive relationships and to understand that changing deep-seated beliefs is often impossible. But if pro-choice and pro-life activists can work together towards developing partnerships among abortion providers and Crisis Pregnancy Centers, preventing teen pregnancy, and promoting adoption, then progress towards fighting poverty, improving healthcare, and promoting a more just culture seems doable.

Let's start by celebrating those elephant riders who are working across differences to get good stuff done while doing our best to ignore those media Talking Heads of Negativity. And let's remember that feelings, not thoughts, drive actions.

A CONVERSATION WITH MAYOR KOCH

February 4, 2013

Today, Ed (How Am I Doing) Koch's funeral service is taking place at an upper east side synagogue, presumably with a boatload of tributes. Here's mine.

Mr. Koch was in the middle of his mayoral reign when I moved to Manhattan. While he was rescuing the city from the brink of irrelevancy, I was barreling through the streets of midtown Manhattan trying to make a name for myself in the music business with assistance from my first guide dog, a weimaraner named Heidi. He continued his reign as I transitioned from an unsuccessful music career to jobs answering phone calls from angry customers at a large federal government agency in Brooklyn and then at a stodgy Wall Street bank.

After leaving his mayoral mantle behind, he started hosting an hour-long talk show on WABC radio, the most listened-to radio station by white males living in the New York City area. His show often served as background noise as I worked towards a master's degree from Columbia University's School of Social Work with the assistance of my second guide dog, a chocolate Lab named Nan. I continued listening as I received my degree and landed a job managing a nationwide project aimed at improving employment opportunities for college students with disabilities.

While I agreed with Mr. Koch's stance on most issues, I became increasingly irritated with his harangues about rap music's vulgarity, descriptions of violence, and contempt for authority. But his biggest complaint was the use of the n-word: that if he used it he would be fired while rappers got a free pass; and that rappers using this word would encourage others to use it.

While sitting at my desk going through paperwork, Mr. Koch once again opened his show with another lecture about the use of the n-word. Annoyed, I snatched up a phone, dialed the station, and somehow got through.

When I got on the air, I thanked Mr. Koch for his work as mayor and told him how much I enjoyed his show. "We agree on many issues," I continued, "but I think you're missing something concerning this n-word thing."

"You know what I say," he simpered, "that if we agree on eight out of twelve issues, we can work together."

"I agree," I told him, and confessed that rappers' use of the n word made me uncomfortable. "I wish they wouldn't do it," I said, "because you're right. It's dehumanizing, and it can send the wrong message to white people."

"So we agree," Mr. Koch interrupted.

"But all groups do this kind of thing," I continued. I told him about how when blind people get together at conventions we often complain about how stupid light-dependent people are, the incompetence of agencies serving us, and the quirks of other blind people. I told him that I had noticed a similar dynamic when social workers and university professionals got together. "I'm sure politicians do it too," I suggested.

Mr. Koch giggled. "Yes, we do — but only in private."

"I agree," I said, "but here's the thing. I hear you make little jokes about Jewish doctors, Jewish lawyers, Jewish accountants, and Jewish mothers on your show."

"But I always say that it's a little joke," he interrupted, an edge to his voice.

"That's true," I said. "And those jokes wouldn't bother me so much if you weren't so ready to label callers as antisemitic when they disagree with you about Israel or other issues related to Judaism."

"But my comments are little jokes, the rappers are being more brazen," he protested.

We spoke for a while about how this complaining within groups brings members closer together while driving others away, and the conversation ended cordially.

Mayor Koch continued to make his little Jewish jokes and to complain about antisemitism until his radio show ended. I'd like to believe that our conversation encouraged him to tone down his act a bit.

Thank you, Mr. Koch, for leading New York City back to the center of the universe. Thank you for your grace and good humor during our conversation. Thanks for reminding us that we don't have to agree on everything to work together.

You've done good.

ROLE REVERSAL

January 20, 2015

While living in New York City in the mid-1990s, news stories of white male police officers shooting African American males as young as ten years old grabbed my attention.

The pattern was drearily predictable. A white policeman/men would shoot a black male because he/they mistook a candy bar, pocket knife, water gun, cell phone, set of keys, or other nonlethal weapon as lethal; or because a black male did something that seemed threatening; or after mistakenly invading the wrong apartment in an attempt to find illegal drugs. White male politicians would insist on media outlets geared towards white men that no judgments be made until the matter was investigated. Columnists and talk show hosts from progressive media sources and on black talk radio would interview friends and/or parents of the victim and criticize what they viewed as institutional racism within the police department. In all but one case, no charges were filed, and in that case, the police officer was acquitted after the trial was moved to a location that white people dominated.

Like most people throughout the political spectrum, I believe that most law enforcement officials do good work, often in difficult environments. Over time, though, I began wondering why only white policemen seem to use excessive force; indeed, I had never heard of a policewoman or African American policeman use excessive force when confronting a white male—

Until January 13, 2015, when I read a column written by John Kass (1).

According to Mr. Kass, the police were called to an assistive living center in July, 2013, to subdue a ninety-five-year-old World War II veteran. The five police officers thought that the shoehorn the veteran was carrying was a machete. The ninety-five-year-old man resisted arrest, and one of the officers fired beanbag rounds at close range, shredding his insides and killing him.

Later in his column, Mr. Kass wrote about his discomfort mentioning that a black policeman had killed that white veteran; that race was irrelevant; and that if the roles had been reversed...

He didn't elaborate.

Dude, everyone is uncomfortable talking about race. And to say race is irrelevant to you concerning this case is silly, as you spend much of your column complaining about how the black-cop-shooting-white-civilian case isn't being publicized as much as recent cases in Ferguson, Missouri and Queens, New York.

Let's bear in mind that police officers' use of excessive force has been a major concern of the African American community, whereas my white friends and I have never expressed a fear of an African American policeman shooting us. Let's also remember that, unlike most of the white policemen using excessive force on black males, justice has the chance to emerge through a trial. Let's also consider that when roles are reversed, media talking heads and activists are required to do something other than regurgitate talking points — often way too difficult for these automatons.

As we reflect on Dr. King's dream that his "four little children will one day live in a nation where they will not be judged by the color of their skin but by the content of their character," it is worth pondering that this character evaluation sometimes takes place in the blink of an eye.

Afterword

A judge acquitted the police officer of all charges (2). I am saddened that an innocent life ended too soon, and continue to wonder why so few officers from underrepresented groups shoot white men in murky circumstances. What can we learn from them?

(1) http://townhall.com/columnists/johnkass/2015/01/13/wwii-vets-death-a-textbook-case-of-excessive-force-but-no-hashtag-for-him-n1942594
(2) http://www.chicagotribune.com/news/local/breaking/ct-wrana-beanbag-shooting-verdict-met-20150204-story.html

RAYS OF LIGHT

August 26, 2015

"Black lives matter!"

"All lives matter!"

"Michael Brown!"

"Darren Wilson!"

"Police crime!"

"Black crime!"

"If police respected us!"

"If you people did what the police told you to do!"

"The blue wall of silence!"

"You're making police ineffective!"

"Discrimination!"

"No fathers!"

"Underfunded schools!"

"You don't care about education!"

"Black lives matter!"

"1,873 black babies murdered every day by abortion!"

Around a year after Michael Brown's death in Ferguson, Missouri, a ray of light penetrated these howls in the darkness.

African American mistrust of law enforcement "is a legitimate issue," senator and presidential candidate Marco Rubio said on a recent appearance on Fox News. "It is a fact that in the African American community around this country, there has been for a number of years now a growing resentment toward how the law enforcement and criminal justice system interacts with the community."

Thanks, Star Parker (1), for bringing Senator Rubio's comments to my attention. Props to Senator Rubio for conveying his thoughts on a media outlet which has been generally hostile towards the views of African Americans. I hope you continue to express these thoughts.

Other promising signs have appeared. Cameras on police car dashboards have encouraged prosecutors to press charges against male police officers who shoot black men without a good reason. Progressive and conservative politicians are working together to pare back some of the criminal justice excesses of the 1990s.

In order to continue the momentum, Black Lives Matter activists might work more with others to develop and implement solutions in addition to protesting injustice. Columnists might convey their suggestions about improving black lives directly to the black community instead of on media outlets viewed primarily by white people who agree with them. Politicians and policy wonks might work across boundaries to develop programs based on the successful work already being done.

Here's to less cursing in the dark and more rays of light.

(1) http://townhall.com/columnists/starparker/2015/08/19/marco-rubio-gets-black-lives-matter-right-n2040474

TWO CONTROVERSY TALES

April 30, 2016

Those of us who live alone while totally blind must find and encourage people to assist us with tasks that involve reading print or driving.

For the past four months, my guide dog and I have been living together in an apartment, and Carol has been buying me groceries, writing the occasional check, sifting through my mostly junk mail, and performing other quirky tasks. We had gotten to know each other as she drove me to and from choir rehearsals during the past couple of years, and it seemed natural for her to assist me in other ways.

We have learned quite a bit about each other. While Carol was raised on a farm with eight brothers and sisters in rural Missouri, I was raised with a younger sister in a village an hour north of New York City. She was once a land-lord; I spent much of my adult life as a tenant. She liked Judge Judy; I liked sports. She liked to cook; I liked to eat. She was still trying to make sense of the death of her only son, and we were both trying to recover from messy relationships.

And we both liked to sing.

One Thursday evening in mid-February, while driving to a rehearsal, Carol stated that she couldn't understand why University of Missouri administrators had forced the president and chancellor to resign because of constant demonstrations of African American students and their allies.

"Why didn't they remove the scholarships from the football players who refused to practice?" she demanded.

I gulped.

"For one thing," I pointed out, "removing the scholarships from football players would make it more difficult to recruit future African American football players."

"I suppose," she growled.

"And I think the Mizzou students are getting too much credit," I continued, "as most faculty members seem to have contempt for both people who were shown the door. The students gave those in power the backbone to do what they should have done a while ago."

A semi-frosty silence lay between us as we walked together from the parking lot to the rehearsal.

On a Tuesday morning about two months later, Carol drove me to an interview for a job involving conducting workshops to strengthen relationship-building skills of people living in poverty. As she was driving me home, she began telling me about one of her former tenants who lived below the poverty line. This tenant received a monthly government check due to some bureaucrat's determination that she had a disability.

"But she didn't seem disabled to me," Carol said.

The government also paid part of the tenant's rent. She either couldn't or wouldn't force her abusive ex-husband to pay child support or look for a job. All she did, Carol told me, was to sit around and smoke cigarettes.

I told her that I had heard similar stories while in social work school and working on a project addressing teenage pregnancy, and that it was hard to know who should take responsibility for what. I talked about a friend who had been diagnosed with traumatic brain injury who was still jumping through hoops four months after applying for benefits.

"But they won't work," Carol insisted.

I pointed out that most people living in poverty had jobs whose salaries kept them dependent on government benefits, and that I couldn't understand why the government allowed corporations like Walmart to get away with this.

"And you know how hard it is for people with disabilities to get jobs," I said.

"But they don't pay taxes."

"I'm one of those people," I told her, "because my family's extraordinarily high medical expenses brings our taxable income to zero."

As I dispensed with my dark suit in my apartment with my guide dog sniffing about, I thought about how shared stories, attentive listening, and a more relaxed vibe had allowed us to unwind the poverty controversy much more effectively than our discussion of the University of Missouri controversy. While I'm certain our basic take on poverty hadn't changed, I believe that our relationship became more solid because we had created a better understanding of the basis for our beliefs.

A week later, Carol died suddenly.

I'll miss her compassionate efficiency, her dry sense of humor, and her willingness to learn from the experiences of others.

Farewell, Carol Huhman; rest in peace.

BOMBAST MATTERS

July 18, 2016

"The Black Lives Matter (BLM) movement is racist! They are at least partially responsible for the deaths of law enforcement officers in Dallas and Baton Rouge! Police officers' behavior around black people is justified because black men are responsible for up to seventy-five percent of all shootings!"

Thus speaks Mayor Rudy Giuliani, Pat Buchanan, Rush Limbaugh, Heather Mac Donald, and others opposed to the movement.

In the 1990s, pro-life advocates (mostly white men) spoke of abortion as murdering unborn babies and compared it to the Holocaust. Attacks against clinics where abortions were performed punctuated news headlines. Protesters shouted "Whore!" "Murderer!" and "You're going to hell!" at women entering clinics. People phoned in threats against clinic employees and volunteers. White men vandalized clinics and killed or wounded doctors and nurses who worked there.

When one of these attacks made headlines, reactions among pro-life spokespeople fell into a pattern. First, a deafening silence, hoping that the media's interest would wane. If pro-choice protests gained traction, pro-life spokespeople would claim that the perpetrator wasn't part of the movement; indeed, I remember Dr. James Dobson of *Focus on the Family* suggesting that pro-abortion activists had committed these acts to make the pro-life side look bad. If that approach failed, pro-life advocates resorted to a brief, muted acknowledgement that the actions were wrong, then explaining in a much louder voice that they were the true victims.

In the late 1990s, I became involved with the project encouraging pro-life and pro-choice activists to dialogue instead of throwing verbal grenades. As these quiet conversations continued, pro-life activists acknowledged how comparing abortion to murder and the holocaust might encourage people to attack clinics, while pro-choice activists grew to accept that almost all pro-life activists opposed these attacks.

The pro-life and BLM movements are both in the less-powerful position trying to affect change related to hot-button issues. It appears that those who attacked clinic staff and police officers were experiencing some sort of mental illness. Some members of each group have used incendiary language: chants of "What do we want? Dead cops! When do we want them? Now!": and "Pigs in a blanket, fry 'em like bacon" at BLM demonstrations, and 1990s pro-lifers use of the phrases "murdering babies" and "the Holocaust." Like pro-life activists in the 1990s, some BLM leaders run from taking responsibility for their movement's incendiary language through silence, denial, and lame apologies. And like many 1990s pro-choice advocates, many BLM opponents refuse to empathize with the concerns of those who disagree with them, hoping that their stridence will silence their opponents. But that tactic hasn't worked with pro-life advocates, and it won't work with BLM advocates either.

I wish that the peacebuilding efforts between leaders of the African American and law enforcement communities that seem to be reducing crime and community complaints were publicized more broadly. I wish that advocates would police the words and actions of their followers before critiquing those with whom they disagree. I wish advocates would understand that bombast will fire up both those who agree and disagree with them.

And that sometimes fire brings forth unpredictable flashes.

TRASH TALK

August 18, 2015

Last week, Bruce Bialosky (1) fooled me with his satiric piece on Townhall. com. His response in a private e-mail was a muted version of the typical put-down so common in the Talkingheadocracy Nation: I'm right, and you're an idiot.

My first reaction was to delete the e-mail. My next thought just prior to falling asleep was that I needed to defend my honor.

The next morning, however, while listening to my wife's gentle breathing, I realized that defending my honor would only play into this I'm-better-than-you game. This game consists of four basic rules:

* The best defense is a good offense;
* I'm the victim, you're the victimizer;
* My intentions are good, yours are not; and
* Trash the other's character as well as their ideas.

When athletes do this, we call it trash-talking, and complain about it, unless it's coming from a player from a team we root for. Talking heads get rewarded in part based on the quality of their trash talk, while the rest of us either cheer or boo depending on whose doing the talking.

Or tune out.

Sports trash-talking, while sometimes amusing, usually turns out to be ineffective because it motivates the other team to rise to the challenge. It's even less effective in developing good-enough solutions. Creative ideas are squelched before they have a chance to bloom. It encourages trash-talkers like Mr. Trump to spew insults instead of solutions. Bureaucracies, whether red, blue, purple, or psychedelic, are more likely to implement ridiculous policies because it's harder to come up with something better when ideologues of all stripes defend their honor via hurling insults.

Take, for example, Mr. Bialosky's (2) second suggestion in his August Ninth Townhall.com article entitled "Pro-Choice But Against Planned Parenthood": eliminate late-term abortions.

Since working with pro-life and pro-choice activists in the late 1990s, I have often wondered if this suggestion could serve as the basis of a grand bargain on abortion. After all, the European Union has by and large made late-term abortions illegal, and many countries have instituted conscience clauses allowing doctors and nurses to opt out of performing abortions. Yet the European rancor around abortion appears much lower than the United States.

I have also wondered what has prevented pro-life activists from using Europe as a talking point in their quest to end abortion. Since most are conservative, perhaps they believe that nothing good can come out of the United Socialist States of Europe. Or they might not want to wrestle with the fact that both the European rate of abortion and teen pregnancy is lower than in the United States despite (or maybe because of) their disconnect from conservative Christianity and orthodox Judaism. The pro-choice activists don't want to change the law because they like the way things are, and, of course, everyone knows that all pro-lifers hate women.

So, abortion activists, to the battlements! Charge! Trash-talk! Fight! Win! Conquer! Kill! Destroy!

Or perhaps some of you could work together behind the scenes to figure out what Europe can teach us about reducing abortion and teen pregnancy while banning late-term abortions.

As for the rest of us, we might try our best to limit the amount of insults we dish out, as well as encouraging more civil conversation from others. We could spend more time supporting those opinion-shapers that focus on solutions instead of spewing insults. My favorites include

Steve Chapman, John Bachelor, Jim Wallis, and Rachel Maddow; what about yours?

(1) http://townhall.com/columnists/brucebialosky/2015/08/02/new-california-law--no-bosses-n2032476

(2) http://townhall.com/columnists/brucebialosky/2015/08/09/prochoice-but-against-planned-parenthood-n2035593

DEAR AMERICAN CONSERVATIVE CHRISTIANS

February 3, 2016

John Hawkins (1), in a column entitled "Dear American Muslims, Can We Have An Honest Talk?", argued that the United States would "be better off doing anything and everything possible to cut back on the number of Muslims we allow to immigrate to our country." He supported this statement through the following points:

* One of his roommates was Muslim;
* While most American Muslims are good, a significant minority support terrorist organizations, jihad, suicide bombings, and/or Sharia law;
* In Europe, so many Muslim immigrants are sexually assaulting women that classes are being organized to tell them that raping women isn't cool; and
* Muslims commit more terrorist attacks and rapes than people from other religious groups.

My response, using this column as a template:

Dear American Conservative Christians:

Over the years, some of you have supported my efforts to make life better for people with disabilities, young adults, and other groups. I believe that most of you are good people; you're opposed to theocratic rule and want to make life better for all of us. I strongly condemn the smearing of all conservative Christians as evil, selfish cretins.

However, a small number of conservative Christians engage in terrorist acts at clinics where abortions are performed, government property, or against fellow Americans who look different, explaining that their Christian faith motivated these actions. More of you tacitly support these actions through excuses, silence, and insincere apologies.

Several of your presidential candidates have taken part in conferences organized by pastors who support theocratic rule and government murder of homosexuals. Some of you believe that Jesus Christ will return soon to kill and send to hell those who disagree with you, and are doing what you can to tinker with the world so that His arrival might be hastened. Obviously, most of you don't support these terrorist acts or destructive beliefs, but many of you seem to think that massive destruction in places where Muslims live will cause extremists in their midst to accept Jesus Christ as their Lord and Savior.

Moreover, look at the alarming increase in sexual assaults on college campuses that have prompted administrators to organize workshops to teach students that it's wrong to rape women. Once again, many of your leaders have blamed the victims and political correctness instead of condemning those who have committed these acts.

The ugly truth is that these problems are specific to fundamentalists of all stripes, and since the United States is freedom's most powerful beacon in the world, our unique brand of fundamentalism rules the roost.

Again, this doesn't mean all conservative Christians are bad. Unfortunately, however, we have proven to be completely incapable of distinguishing moderate conservative Christians from radicals. If you think we can distinguish between John, the freedom-loving good citizen, from John, the wannabe terrorist who dreams of blowing up government buildings, your ears are still ringing from lousy praise-the-Lord music.

Because of our inability to screen out radicals, we'd be better off encouraging conservative Christians to immigrate to environments more hospitable to their beliefs. We should offer financial incentives for these malcontents to move to Russia, Liberia, Zaire, or other countries that support the persecution of homosexuals and Muslims. Of course, we shouldn't force anyone to leave against their will, but we should try to minimize the number of conservative Christians who live among us.

We should be prepared to accept reality as opposed to what we wish it should be. It's time for us to deal realistically with the significant minority of American conservative Christians who wish to destroy our culture by any means necessary.

(1) http://townhall.com/columnists/johnhawkins/2016/02/02/dear-american-muslims-can-we-have-an-honest-talk-n2113364

OUR BETTER ANGELS

September 6, 2016

As the controversy surrounding Colin Kaepernick's refusal to stand during the playing of the United States' national anthem continues to swirl, I can't help but wonder how well "The Star-Spangled Banner" reflects our country's better angels.

Francis Scott Key, the anthem's lyricist, was a well-connected, prosperous lawyer. John Stafford Smith, a Brit, composed the tune, which became the official song of an eighteenth-century gentlemen's club of amateur musicians. (No wonder it's so hard to sing!) The text of the first three verses describes the heroism of United States troops during various battles while our flag forever waved, while the fourth verse describes how Warrior God supports our efforts "when our cause it is just."

President George W. Bush called us peace-loving people. How well does our national anthem represent this side of our character?

Then there's "America the Beautiful." Katharine Lee Bates, college professor and poet, wrote the lyrics, which speak of our diverse geography, "pilgrim feet", the heroic sacrifice of those who have protected us, and our gleaming cities. Throughout the poem, she characterized God as a gracious, merciful, and just healer. Samuel A. Ward, a United States citizen, composed the music.

And what about Irving Berlin's prayer-song "God Bless America?" And Woody Guthrie's more secular "This Land Is Your Land?"

Mountains. Prairies. Oceans. Rivers. Villages. Cities.

Builders. Protectors. Laborers. Artists. Teachers. Healers. Businesspeople. Farmers. Bureaucrats. Preachers.

Such diversity. Such challenges and opportunities. Yet our national anthem trumpets only part of who we are.

So why not vary the patriotic tunes during sporting events? Why not encourage students in civics or history classes to reflect on how these songs highlight different parts of our character?

As for the Colin Kaepernick kerfuffle, I suggest that all sides acknowledge that Colin has the right to protest in any peaceful way he chooses, and that actions speak louder than talk. I also suggest that conservative Christians support Colin and his supporters kneeling instead of sitting during the playing of the national anthem, as their radio spokespeople stress the importance of praying for our country. I encourage people from all sides to publicize efforts in Dallas, Texas; Stockton, California; and other places throughout the country where police-community partnerships are reducing both crime and complaints against law enforcement officers.

We can go a long way towards addressing these challenges if we let our better angels prevail.

"America! America!

God shed His grace on thee,

And crown thy good with brotherhood

From sea to shining sea!"

PART VI

MUSIC

Where I reflect on how my early music experiences shaped my life; highlight the influence of several musicians that have crossed my path; and point to some connections between music and the world around us.

ONE OF THOSE

January 22, 2017

"How do you memorize the music that choir directors throw your way even though you're blind?" many people have asked me with awe in their voices.

I never quite know how to answer such questions, as I don't think what I do is particularly awe-inspiring or interesting. I usually deflect the question with humor, promising to write about it in a future blog post.

So...how do I remember all that music?

When I started singing in choirs nearly forty-five years ago, choral music in braille didn't exist, so I had to learn everything by ear. I wasn't sure I really wanted to sing, but I did want to play drums in the marching band. As the adults in charge thought I might be able to sing but couldn't march, my best shot to be accepted in the band was to do well in the choir since the same man conducted both groups.

But learning the music was not all that hard because, thanks to my mother, I had been exposed to music of varying styles through recordings. I also took piano lessons, which, because of the quirks of braille music notation, forced me to learn about the structure of intervals and chords. I had to memorize everything I played, since my hands couldn't be in two places at once. Playing the drums also sharpened my ability to connect rhythms with music styles. So memorizing one choral line, even without braille music, was simple, almost relaxing.

In high school, my involvement with the marching band, pickup rock groups, church music ensembles, and Broadway pit orchestras sharpened my music intelligence. Along the way, I worked with several terrific musicians who took time to mentor me. As I moved into college and young adulthood, composing music became an increasingly important part of my life.

Today, when confronted with a new piece of music, my first goal is to determine the style in which it is written. Baroque? Classical? Romantic? Jazz? Contemporary classical? Americana? Top forty? World music? Gospel? Modal? Something else?

"Oh, it's one of those," I catch myself saying once the style becomes clear. Then I can predict with some certainty the way my choral part will connect with the harmony and the structure of the piece based on my prior experience. Of course, I make many mistakes at the beginning, but being wrong gets my attention, and over time, I'm more likely to get it right.

Like skilled cyclists, skateboarders, and race car drivers, I've learned how to benefit from the energy that comes from being the proper distance from something that's more powerful. Sitting or standing next to a stronger singer not only speeds up the learning process, but also prepares me for a conductor's cue that I can't see.

Then, there's the Lewin effect.

Kurt Lewin, one of the founders of social psychology, was famous for conducting experiments on the fly, which he later called action research. According to one of my mentors, one of these ad hoc experiments took place at an outdoor cafe where Mr. Lewin hung out with a group of his students. A server would take coffee-pastry orders without writing anything down — and give each person what he or she asked for.

Every time.

Without ever making a mistake.

One day, immediately after the waiter had flawlessly completed another complicated order, Dr. Lewin offered the waiter a large amount of money if he could remember what each person had ordered — without looking, of course.

The waiter couldn't do it.

The same is true for me. Usually, several days after a performance, the music I've memorized recedes into a cranny of my brain. Like the waiter, I need to clear some space in order to fill it with something new.

So, it's all about pattern recognition, being a good follower, and clearing some mental space after a performance in order to start again.

I never thought that forgetting might be a critical part of remembering. It must be one of those ...

IT WAS FIFTY YEARS AGO

June 13, 2017

My relationship with the Beatles got off on the wrong foot when a relative living in Great Britain sent me the album *Rubber Soul* as a Christmas present. As an eight-year-old kid, I had no opinion about the band, except vague annoyance that screeching girls often made it hard to hear their songs. Since classical music was the primary music heard around our house, I thought that it was politically incorrect to like the Beatles.

"I hate the Beatles!" I declared.

It turned out I was wrong, as Mom began regularly playing the record.

My connection with the band really started when I heard their song "Eight Days a Week" on the school bus surrounded by older kids. The tune was catchy, and while I didn't care about the meaning of love, the idea that someone could be committed enough to do something for more than 168 hours per week was intriguing. During the next eighteen months, I began developing a taste for top 40 tunes, including "Michelle", "Hard Day's Night", "Yellow Submarine", "Ticket to Ride", and "Penny Lane."

In early June, 1967, my sister and I were eating dinner in our stuffy kitchen with the radio nearby playing the first three songs from the recently-released *Sgt. Pepper's Lonely Hearts Club Band* album.

I was totally confused. Who was Sergeant Pepper? What was with those French horns and audience laughter? Who was that weird dude singing about "getting high with a little help from my friends?" Weren't drugs bad? Who was "Lucy in the Sky with Diamonds?" What was with all those weird lyrics and musical effects?

Life continued. Two months at a camp with military overtones. "Good

Morning Good Morning." A snap decision to focus my music energies away from the piano to the drums. "Lovely Rita." Increased immersion into pop music and rock and roll. "Fool on the Hill"; "Strawberry Fields Forever"; and "All You Need Is Love." Increased homework. "When I'm Sixty Four." My Mom and dad moving towards divorce. "She's Leaving Home."

In June, 1968, I attended another two-month camp, this one without military overtones. One morning, my counselor and I were alone listening to "A Day in the Life." The lyrics and music, although weird, sounded somehow OK.

"Strange," I said aloud after listening to the second improvisatory orchestral ascension to the stratosphere.

"Watch out!" the counselor warned.

And as that final deep chord faded into silence, something seemed a little better within and without. At that moment, I sensed that music didn't need to neatly fit into just one category: that styles could be mixed and matched to create a wondrous joyful noise.

Something I'm still exploring fifty years later.

FASCINATING METERS

April 13, 2017

Throughout grammar school, I took piano lessons, and most of the classical music I played was in four-four time, with a few pieces in three-four and six-eight time. In fifth grade, I ditched the piano for the drums, and again most of the rock and jazz pieces I learned were in four-four time, with a few pieces in three-four and six-eight time. This became dull.

In seventh grade, while listening for the first time to Andrew Lloyd Weber's and Tim Rice's rock opera *Jesus Christ Superstar* with a friend who had just started high school, I noticed that some of the music sounded rhythmically weird. In a bored voice, my friend told me that the song to which we were listening was in five-four time, and that a later song was in seven-four time.

When I mentioned this discovery to my drum teacher, he played me the second movement of Tchaikovsky's Sixth Symphony, pointing out its five-four meter.

I was fascinated.

Not by Tchaikovsky, whose music is a bit too bombastic for my taste, but by these unusual time signatures.

But most of my musical mentors throughout high school and college didn't quite know what to make of my interest in these meters. They kept trying to steer me into writing music using more traditional meters, arguing that no one would be able to play music that didn't use traditional time signatures. These mentors became further dismayed when I discovered how composers used different time signatures throughout the same piece of music.

I cheerfully ignored much of this advice. After all, Stravinsky, Copeland, Bartok, Bernstein, BRUBECK, Sondheim, the Beatles, Pink Floyd, Jethro Tull, and many other composers/arrangers used unusual meters to great effect, so why couldn't I? So I experimented, and most performers rose to the challenge without much fuss.

Unless they were affiliated with elite music conservatories.

One summer, while attending a festival for elite musicians, I asked the jazz ensemble to read a piece I had composed. It was harmonically straightforward, but much of it was written in five-four time, with a couple of eleven-eight measures thrown in. Mutinous muttering swelled as the parts were handed out, and while they did read through the piece, we parted on dissonant terms. Yet a year later, a university jazz band consisting of only one music major (me) performed the piece with great gusto in front of an enthusiastic audience.

Shortly after the turn of the millennium, I arranged an American folk tune in seven-eight time for a pick-up choir of visually-impaired singers. After introducing myself and the piece to the audience, I asked the audience for their patience as I conveyed a message to the choir.

"One-two one-two one-two-three one-two one-two one-two-three," I chanted into the microphone.

Everyone laughed, and the piece went well.

Since moving to Columbia, Missouri, I have sung in four choirs. Conductors are far more conversant with musical styles ranging from traditional and contemporary classical to jazz and gospel. They find ways to connect warm-up exercises to the music we're learning to sing. And they are more confident around unusual meters.

This confidence communicates to the singers. During last Monday's rehearsal of a choir that requires no audition to join, the conductor, in a matter-of-fact voice, introduced us to a portion of a piece we will be performing this summer.

"One-two one-two one-two-three one-two one-two one-two-three," she chanted, and we launched into the section as if this rhythm was an old friend.

Which, for many of us, it now is.

BANGING THE DRUM LOUDLY

October 3, 2012

My campaign to join the high school marching band began in the spring of 1971 when my mother and I met with the high school's guidance counselor. I was an eighth-grader at a local private school where I was the only student who was blind. My mom had decided that the local high school would serve my education and social needs better.

"What do you enjoy doing?" the guidance counselor chirped.

"I play the drums," I mumbled.

"Great!" she said, and began rattling off all of the musical possibilities: the chorus, the marching band—"

"I want to be in the band," I interrupted.

"You can't do that," she barked.

I didn't argue because Mom had stressed the importance of making a good impression. "They're still not sure they'll accept you," she had warned earlier.

I spent my freshman year adjusting to the new school where again I was the only blind student. I took a full load of courses and began the frustrating process of making friends.

Toward the end of my freshman year, I told the band conductor that I was planning to join the marching band the following year as a drummer.

"But how will you learn the music?" the conductor spluttered.

"That'll be easy, Mr. V. I can learn the stuff by ear."

"And how will you march?"

"I have no idea, but I'm sure we can work things out."

I joined the band the following fall, and learning the music by ear was easy. But performing the simplest maneuvers in step with the rest of the band was impossible. Connecting me by rope with another percussionist caused us both to become entangled as the rest of the band tried to maneuver around us.

Fortunately, Mr. V., instead of giving up, suggested that I stand with him during the halftime maneuvering and that someone could run with me to the percussion section after the completion of the formation but before they started playing, and then run me back to him as the band started its next marching routine. While I wasn't totally happy with this arrangement, my experience playing with neighborhood kids had taught me that I didn't have to do everything that sighted people did to be accepted. I was having fun and making friends while making a real contribution.

I overcame the barrier of not being able to march with the band during my senior year. This was important because the best drummer was supposed to teach the various cadences we used as the band marched to our rhythm, call the cadence changes, communicate Mr. V.'s sometimes confusing instructions, and generally keep the section together. Everybody agreed that I was the person for the job, except that I couldn't march.

"For Heaven's sake," Mom said after listening to my dilemma, "why don't you find someone to grab your elbow and steer you from behind?"

Mom's solution worked brilliantly. Mr. V. found a female volunteer, and I was soon strutting with the band shouting directions over the noise of the drums while she discreetly kept me in line with subtle tugs on my elbow and whispered directions in my ear. This solution worked even better while in college since its marching band considered drinking alcohol from concealed flasks while sitting in the stands and writing sexually charged scripts that were read during the halftime show to be more important than marching in lockstep to create fancy formations.

Looking back, I realize how fortunate I was to have the chance to bang the drums loudly in the band. It taught me the power of working together to make a joyful noise. It taught me the value of collaborating with others to find solutions to overcome barriers. Most importantly, the skills and confidence I developed while leading a group of sighted people to accomplish something worthwhile have proved invaluable in my work assisting groups and organizations to become more effective. I thank now-Dr. V., my mother, and my fellow band members for giving me the chance to have fun, to struggle, and then to succeed.

REQUIEM REMEMBRANCES

June 1, 2015

While growing up, my mother made sure that I was exposed to all kinds of music: Vivaldi, Bach, Beethoven, Gershwin, and Menotti; cast recordings of *Oliver*, *The Music Man*, and *West Side Story*; and songs of Pete Seeger, Simon and Garfunkel, the Beatles, and the Doors.

While taking part in a recent rehearsal of Mozart's *Requiem*, it occurred to me that this composition was one of Mom's favorite pieces of music, yet I didn't remember her including this music on her play list. I did remember, though, that her two sisters and she would sing an impromptu version of the first several phrases of the "Rex Tremendae" movement after drinking several glasses of wine.

I sent Mom an e-mail asking about her memories about the connection between Mozart's *Requiem* and my growing-up years. She responded, in part:

"I must have played the Mozart for you. I just don't remember doing it. ... But one thing I know for sure, it was not wine, it was whiskey that we drank, lots of it."

But I have no memory of hearing a recording of the *Requiem* in our house until one dreary late winter afternoon of my sophomore year in high school. I was in my room pretending to do homework when I heard the "Domine Jesu" that starts the second half of the work. I recognized the piece because I had overheard my organ teacher telling someone else that the background music he was playing while driving us home from a field trip was a recording of him conducting the piece.

I sat spellbound drinking in the fugue-like passages and the double fugue that serves both as the second and last movements of the work; the unusual harmonies for music of that period; and the weird false cadences. The concluding neither-major-or-minor chord was the final hook.

Last October, my then sixteen-year-old stepson started talking about how bored he was with the melody-chord progression techniques he was learning in his advanced placement music theory class.

"Isn't there more to music than that?" he asked.

"Of course," I told him, "there's counterpoint."

"What's that?"

I explained that a good deal of music focused on how melodies that individual voices play or sing come together to suggest a chord progression instead of ramming the progression down the listener's throat.

"Do you have an example?" he asked.

I said the first thing that came to mind. "The second movement of the Mozart *Requiem.*"

"The what?" he asked.

"I have it on CD downstairs. I'll let you know when I find it."

"Don't worry," he told me as I headed to the stairs, "I can find it on my iPad."

"Is this it?" my stepson called a couple of minutes later.

"Yes!" I said, astounded that he had found the piece so quickly.

Although the version he had found sounded like it had been performed by a herd of stomping elephants, I could tell that my stepson, like me, had been mesmerized. Shortly afterwards, he began composing pieces more linearly than chordally, much to my delight and his teacher's consternation.

REMEMBERING JANIECE

June 9, 2013

Since 1985, I have been a member of the American Council of the Blind (ACB for short), whose mission is to improve living conditions for people with visual impairments. Several years later, I joined Friends-in-Art (FIA), a small group of blind musicians, writers, sculptors, painters, and others who try to advance accessibility and opportunity for artists and audience members who are visually impaired. We encourage museums to become more blind-friendly and work with designers of popular music-related hardware and software to make their products more user-friendly for blind musicians. We also conduct several workshops at ACB's annual national conventions, as well as putting on a popular variety show.

During that time, I got to know Janiece Kent, a talented pianist/vocalist with a special affinity for show tunes and operetta arias; a gifted poet; a teacher of braille to blind students in the Washington, DC school system; a tireless advocate — and a founding member of FIA.

In the late 1990s, I moved to an apartment in Washington, DC about a mile from Janiece. My guide dogs and I spent many happy afternoons and evenings with her and Gordon, her future husband, in their apartment. She was a gracious and unassuming host with kind words, a listening ear, and a sense of humor that often caught me by surprise. She sang the women's parts when I recorded demos of my music in Gordon's studio, often singing them correctly on the first take despite not having the time to review the material beforehand.

Janiece played a pivotal role in my courtship of my wife, Lisa. I sang to Lisa and others attending a FIA variety show Stephen Sondheim's "Not

While I'm Around" with her accompanying on the piano. Lisa and I heard her perform several times at the Old Europe, a German restaurant near my DC apartment. She teamed with Gordon to sing two Broadway show tunes at our wedding, causing many people to turn in their seats expecting a recording but seeing live performers instead.

I will especially remember Janiece's unique approach to making herself heard during meetings. She was no longer FIA's president when I joined the board, but she was always present with perceptive comments and wise suggestions ... if we gave her the space.

Giving Janiece that space took some practice, especially when we were under pressure to create a program for the annual variety show in ninety minutes after listening to auditions over a three-hour period. She would attempt to change the tone of the rapid, impatient conversation in which the rest of us were engaged with a quiet but distinct "excuse me," coupled with her clearing her throat. If we didn't give her the chance to speak, she might or might not try to interrupt us again several seconds later. If she got our attention, she would clear her throat again, pause, and then make her comment in a quiet, slow voice. If she didn't get our attention, we lost the benefit of her wisdom. Over time, I learned to listen for her gentle but insistent cue that she wanted to say something.

This unique approach to getting heard has assisted me to become better at running meetings and workshops, especially when the tone becomes contentious. I have tried to do a better job of picking up cues from people with quieter voices so that they can have their say. When people's agitation causes them to talk past each other, I have consciously slowed down my rate of speech, often resulting in others following my lead and more productive work getting done.

Thanks, Janiece, for your gracious hospitality. Thanks for your wonderful music, your love of poetry, and your enthusiasm for everything artistic. Thanks for your efforts to make museums, concerts, and films more friendly to us blind people. Thanks for doing such a terrific job teaching braille to blind kids in the wildly dysfunctional DC public school system. Thanks for assisting me to become a better teacher and leader. And thanks for showing us that friendship can produce not just great art but also positive change in the world around us.

RIP, Janiece Kent)

TEA

March 16, 2016

Choir culture confuses.

Women and men divide themselves into four groups, except that one of the men's groups sometimes includes women. The women's groups call themselves sopranos (sops for short) and altos, while the mixed-gender group call themselves tenors and the all-men's group call themselves basses.

Idle chatter ceases when someone calling herself or himself a conductor asks participants to stand and participate in such adult activities as Follow the Leader, making silly noises, and waving their arms.

Then come exercises designed to warm up the voice. Members might be asked to sing a prearranged ascending series of tones, with each ascending tone assigned a higher number. That seems easy to those steeped in choir culture, but problems emerge when the conductor asks that clapping or foot-stomping substitute for given tones. Worse yet, sometimes words from the Broadway hit show "The Sound of Music" take the place of numbers.

"Doe, a deer, a female deer;

Ray, a drop of golden sun" ...

Ending with

"Tea, we drink with jam and bread; That will bring us back to"

A female deer?

Throughout these warm-up activities, conductors ask members to imagine that they are sequoia trees or that they are eating apples.

Then, the real work of the organization begins when, under the guidance of the conductor, members learn to translate squiggles on pieces of paper into pleasant and unpleasant sounds. (Unless you are in something called a gospel choir, in which case squiggly lines are abandoned and the members learn their parts by ear via conductor vocal prompts.)

Now imagine what might happen if the being unfamiliar with choir culture is a service animal named Heath. Being a guide dog, he is trained to handle a variety of cultural differences by lying quietly by my feet. (My first guide dog, a weimaraner named Heidi, would occasionally complain loudly if choir culture norms didn't conform to her sense of decorum, but Heath, a black Lab, is more tolerant.)

Heath has learned to stand up and shake himself whenever I rise up out of a chair while in public. As choir conductors ask us to rise out of our chairs at unpredictable times, he has had to learn to sleep through these sudden uprisings.

But choir cultural quirks can yield even weirder reactions.

Conductors occasionally ask members to substitute nonsense syllables for words on those pieces of paper — syllables such as "ta", "doe" (what's this obsession with female deer?), and "tea."

Recently, Heath raised his head while "teas" at various rates and pitches were cascading around him.

"It's OK," I said, putting my hand on his head, but he continued to remain alert.

"You know what the problem is?" my neighbor asked quietly after we stopped teaing.

"No," I said, mystified.

My neighbor laughed. "He thinks we're calling his name."

"Tea? Heath?" I wondered aloud.

I think my neighbor was right.

Heath has learned to sleep through these cultural confusions by a mixture of sound training augmented by reassuring words and pats on the head. We humans can bridge culture differences through a blend of patience, humor, empathy, and clear communication from both cultural insiders and outsiders. If we're successful, we can transform female deer, squiggly lines, and tea into beautiful music.

THE VIBRANT POETS SOCIETY

October 27, 2014

Last summer, I received a commission to compose a piece that a small choir would perform the following March.

"What text should I set to music?" I wondered.

My first thought was to reach out to poets with disabilities, given that 2015 would be the twenty-fifth anniversary of the Americans with Disabilities Act. So I sent an e-mail to all my artist friends and colleagues with a connection to disability, yielding only one poem after a month.

"That didn't work," I harumphed.

So I asked the choir's conductor if we could reach out to the local high schools to encourage students to submit poems for me to set. One thing led to another, and ten days ago, the conductor, her infant, my guide dog, and I visited a group of fifth-graders at Lee Elementary School, a magnet school that focuses on the arts.

About a month earlier, I had e-mailed my thoughts concerning the requirements of a poem that could be effectively set to music to a teacher at Lee.

"The poem can be of any style and cover any topic," I had written. "Something short (less than twelve lines) describing a feeling using unusual images, that plays with words, and/or uses a repeated phrase would be ideal."

The kids were calm but excited as the four of us sidled to the front of the room.

After brief introductions, the teacher asked the six students — all girls — who had written poems to read them aloud. Each read their poem quickly but clearly. The poems were short and full of forward motion, with themes ranging from the meaning of life, friendship, and exploration to tolerance, effort, and springtime.

"These are great!" I told the kids. "I hope you remember that the poems I don't choose aren't any better or worse than the poem or poems I decide to set; it merely means that the `winning` poems speak to me more musically than the others."

After briefly showing them my computer with a Braille display and talking about my guide dog and life as a musician/organization psychologist, I asked the conductor to say a few words.

"I don't talk; I do," the conductor declared. "Please stand."

The kids jumped to their feet.

"Now, watch me, and repeat what I do."

Within ninety seconds, the kids were singing the French nursery rhyme "Frere Jacques", accompanied by hand-clapping, foot-stomping, and finger-snapping. It was a bravura performance that adult choirs would have a hard time matching.

After this ad hoc performance, I introduced the march I had written to celebrate my marriage to Lisa. (1)

"The piece was scored for brass and percussion," I explained, "but recorded on a keyboard that had pretty good brass and percussion sounds."

"Those kids were incredible," I told the conductor as she drove my guide dog and me home. "Full of focused energy."

Growing up, my involvement with music provided me with an array of skills that have served me well leading groups, raising stepkids, and herding two standard poodles and my guide dog. Studies have reinforced the skillbuilding effects when incorporating arts education into the standard reading, writing, math, science, and foreign language curriculum. My visit with those fifth-grade students highlighted the power of the arts in growing young minds.

I have yet to decide which poem or poems to set, but I'm thinking about clarinets.

Afterword

I ended up setting two of the poems for choir and solo clarinet: "Our Friendship's Like a Rainbow," written by Yada Olson; and "Spring Morning," written by Emily Williams. The pieces were performed during a concert six months later; everybody, especially the poets, seemed pleased.

(1) For those interested in hearing this piece, please go to http://www.peteraltschul.com/book-related-information/ and look for the piece entitled *"Festive (Wedding) Recessional* (2007)." Please be patient, as it takes a while to load.)

MYSTERY OF THE DEAD

July 19, 2015

Lisa is a devout Deadhead, having attended thirty Grateful Dead concerts during a ten-year period. My contact with the Dead was primarily based on the songs that album-oriented radio stations played. I wasn't impressed.

About three months ago, Lisa heard about the Dead's final three concerts in Chicago. She felt a calling to go; I did not.

In late June, Lisa noticed that ticket prices on StubHub were decreasing rapidly, and two days before the first concert, she finagled two free nights lodging at the Chicago Hilton, seven-tenths of a mile from the concert venue.

"I need a miracle every day," Lisa chortled, quoting the title of one of the Dead's more famous songs.

I grumbled incoherently.

So we headed to Chicago, our trunk loaded with everything we would need to enjoy the weekend on a limited budget and with Grateful Dead music playing on our SiriusXM car radio. During the eight-hour trip, I complained about the band's inability to sing in tune.

"It all depended on what extracurricular activities the band took part in prior to performing," Lisa explained.

"At best," I continued, "they're a diluted version of the Allman Brothers, and, at worst, they sound like that dreadful Lynyrd Skynyrd Band's song `FreeBird`"

But there were unpredictable times when Dead vocals sounded good, and even rarer moments when their voices sounded good together. I also began to appreciate the quality of their songs, which often told stories and featured quirky rhythms. They incorporated aspects of bluegrass, country, southern gospel, blues, reggae, disco, and jazz into their music. Their improvisations, especially those connected with their "drums and space" concert segments, reminded me of my improvisations on pipe organs in high school and in contemporary ensembles in graduate school.

"But they still can't sing," I grumbled in the middle of a traffic jam two blocks from the hotel.

As Lisa and I entered the elevator, I smelled something out of place.

"Is that scent what I think it is?" I asked.

"What. Pot?" she said, laughing.

"That's what I thought."

"These are Deadheads, dear," she reminded me.

Over the weekend, I became acquainted with aspects of Deadhead culture. They loved ingesting interesting plants, and were supportive of those experiencing the unwelcomed side effects. Almost all conversations featured some version of "yeah, man" or "thanks, man."

Deadheads were enthusiastically inept at giving clear directions. Lisa and I spent an hour wandering aimlessly on a warm, windy afternoon looking for a Starbucks based on Deadhead directions even though three were located within four blocks of the hotel. (It didn't help that I am totally blind while she is legally blind, and that we were both hung over).

The Deadheads were totally in sync with the band. They roared when familiar riffs sounded forth. They joyously sang along to songs familiar to them but not to me, remembering the complex lyrics and being unfazed by the quirky rhythms. They raved about the quality of the improvisations.

The improvisations were indeed awe-inspiring, often more interesting than the songs themselves. The "drums and space" segments incorporated live and prerecorded music. In short, the Dead had morphed into a fusion jazz ensemble with electrifying results. And the vocals? Better than usual.

"Wow!" I kept saying, smiling from ear to ear. "Totally awesome!"

"I told you so," Lisa said with a smile in her voice.

After the last concert's two encores, I remember one of the Grateful Dead members approaching the microphone to thunderous applause.

"Be kind," he said, and walked off to renewed applause.

I learned later that Mickey Hart was the one who spoke. As summarized in *The New York Times* (1):

"The feeling we have here — remember it, take it home and do some good with it," Mr. Hart said in closing. "I'll leave you with this: Please, be kind."

The Deadheads were kind to each other and to strangers. Several hotel staff commented that they were the nicest customers they had served.

As for the band itself, I still find much of their music uneven, and their vocals cringe-inducing. At their best, they shine a great light. They have built a community consisting of all ages and ethnic backgrounds and taken them on a wild, wonderful, kind, and joyful journey through a wide range of musical styles. I'm blessed to be part of the last three shows of that journey.

(1) https://artsbeat.blogs.nytimes.com/2015/07/06/the-grateful-dead-close-out-their-final-concert-with-words-please-be-kind-amid-tears-and-hugs/

HOOKED ON MARTY

September 21, 2016

In high school and college, I sang in several choirs, each led by talented, well-organized conductors. I currently sing in four choirs with equally talented, organized conductors, and appreciate their leadership as they steer us volunteer singers towards performing repertoire in wide-ranging styles.

And then there was Marty.

I first met Marty several years ago when he took charge of the Agape Singers, a church choir that sings contemporary Christian music. I wasn't sure what to make of him. He never started rehearsals with warm-up exercises, a staple of all other conductors I have worked with. His rehearsals often seemed to border on chaos. University music students made snarky comments about the way he conducted.

"But what makes him so successful?" I asked one of these students, an up-and-coming choral conductor as noises of a chamber orchestra enveloped us with sound. "I mean, most of us aren't the most talented musicians in the universe, yet we sing a different contemporary Christian piece each week and team up with the other church choir to sing more traditional pieces by Bach, Handel, Vivaldi, Durufle, Rutter, and other contemporary classical composers."

"I don't know," she said, taken aback.

I'm not sure I know either, but here are some thoughts.

Marty was the only conductor I have met who could talk with intelligent enthusiasm about all musical styles, from chant song to Brahms to contemporary Top Forty pop tunes. I walked into one Sunday morning rehearsal as Marty and several college students were discussing the merits of current Grammy-award winning songs. He premiered three of my compositions, and his command of musical styles allowed him to instinctually grasp what I was trying to accomplish through my music.

But I never fully appreciated Marty's interest in diverse musical styles until I told him that Lisa and I had attended the concluding Grateful Dead concerts in Chicago. His voice lit up as we discussed the mix of talents, grit, and flaws that made the Dead come to life.

Much of choral arrangements of Christian contemporary music are sonically malnourishing, but Marty always chose satisfying pieces for us to sing. Even when I didn't like the style of a given piece, I knew that what we were singing was well-crafted, which motivated me to do my best each week.

While he seemed to have little patience with traditional rehearsal-leading techniques, Marty's easygoing style made each weekly forty-five minute rehearsal fly by. He spent little time pounding out voice parts on the piano, expecting the stronger singers in each voice part to lead the rest of us.

Marty was the essence of servant leadership: always humble; always interested in strengthening others; always willing to do those menial, boring tasks to keep things moving. And his quiet, confident joy was ever present, especially towards the end of his time with us.

Three days after Marty announced his retirement due to medical issues, he sang the anthem at the following Sunday's church service, probably because no one else had volunteered. To my ears, the piece he sang was dreadful, yet he communicated a sense of joyful faith through a weak and warbly voice. He died peacefully two weeks later.

Thanks, Marty, for reminding me that the athletic coach style with the brassy voice and type A personality doesn't always make the best leader; that a calm, confident, nurturing servant leadership style can often yield comparable, sometimes better, results.

RIP, Marty Hook.

CHEESY CORN

May 30, 2016

Last night, about sixteen of us performed during a banquet honoring military personnel throughout the United States and Canada. We sang what our conductor called cheesy arrangements of "This Land Is Your Land"; "Flanders Field"; and "The Battle Hymn of the Republic", along with the Canadian and American national anthems.

Growing up, I didn't like cheese, unless it was part of a grilled cheese sandwich (called toasted cheese sandwich in Missouri). The word "cheese" was also associated with one of my least favorite activities: being part of a picture-taking session.

I made fun of cheesy music arrangements beginning when I was four years old, although the word we used in New York was "corny." Slow pop tunes of the 1930s, 1940s, and 1950s with lush orchestrations and saxophones prompted snarky comments and loud snores. This behavior caused hurt feelings from pastors and my grandmother, as well as angry comebacks from teachers and conductors.

"The piece is horrible," Mom would tell me, "but you can't say it aloud, and you can't fall asleep."

I now love cheese, except perhaps the really smelly, pungent kinds. As for picture-posing, I try to get through it with grace and humor.

And cheesy music?

Everybody has a different take on how to define this genre. For some, it's the music our parents liked while they were growing up. For others, it's music of a certain style.

For me, cheesy music is comfort music. It's the music that served as the soundscape of our lives when we were happy and relaxed. It's the slow dance song played at our senior proms. It's the song sung at our weddings. It's the familiar tunes we hear during religious services. It's the music played during graduations and holidays. Barry Manilow, The Carpenters, Lionel Richie, Kenny Rogers, Celine Dion, and Mariah Carey? All exemplars of the genre, especially their ballads. "White Christmas?" The pinnacle of cheesy greatness.

I've learned "Through the Years" (a Kenny Rogers tune that qualifies as lousy corny music) that this music can be wonderful. It's often the arrangement — how a song is showcased — that can make it shine or drown in a cheesy, corny goo.

Familiar patriotic music is corny. It's comforting. It reminds us of who we are. It brings us together. It provides cues about what makes us good and how we can get better.

YACHT ROCK

September 25, 2015

Last week, Lisa and I celebrated our eighth wedding anniversary at home "Reminiscing" (Little River Band) while consuming brie in puffed pastry, California rolls, and sparkling wine with background music, courtesy of SiriusXM radio.

"You're listening to Yacht Rock radio," the announcer intoned in a snarky, pompous voice, along with patter about the minimum size of a boat before it could be properly called a yacht.

"Yacht what?" Lisa asked with a smile in her voice, accompanied by the thunk of a glass gently being placed on the table.

I explained that ten years ago, a couple of people put together a series of video spoofs about the incestuous (symbiotic?) collaborations in the late 1970s and early 1980s between Michael McDonald ("Shine, Sweet Freedom") of the Doobie Brothers ("What A Fool Believes") and Steely Dan ("Hey Nineteen"), Hall and Oates ("Kiss On My List"), Toto (Rosanna"), Kenny Loggins ("This Is It"), and Christopher Cross (Sailing").

"I'm not quite sure what qualifies as Yacht Rock," I added. "But the production is always clean. The vocalists sing clearly. There's often a jazz influence, as well as a certain sophistication in the arrangements. It's soft but not hard-core soft; Barry Manilow doesn't make the cut. It also helps if the lyrics have some sort of maritime or weather connection."

"I'm bored," Lisa said after a while. "Can we listen to the Grateful Dead Channel?"

"Of course," I said, switching to another type of yuppie music.

According to SiriusXM experts, George "Give Me the Night" Benson,

Al "We're in This Love Together" Jarreau, the "Long Run" Eagles, Lionel "You Are" Richie, Little "Cool Change" River Band, and Rupert "Him" Holmes make the cut, but Michael Jackson and Earth, Wind and Fire don't. (I'm not sure why, but whatever.)

In college and at the Aspen Music Festival, I learned about the inner workings of compositions by Monteverdi, Bach, Mozart, Beethoven, Brahms, Liszt, Debussy, Berg, Hindemeth, Stravinsky, Babbitt, and others. While in graduate school, I learned about the techniques of contemporary classical composition and jazz arranging. At the same time, I listened to Yacht Rock, mixed with R&B (Earth, Wind, and Fire), guitar-centric rock (Journey), and country-pop songs (Kenny Rogers) with my nonmusician friends while drinking beer, lounging by bodies of water, or just hanging out. My musician friends told me that I was selling out, while my nonmusician friends accused me of being a music snob. Perhaps they were both right.

Nonetheless, those Yacht Rock tunes served as a Northern Star (Gerry Raffertty's "Right Down the Line") and an "Escape", (Rupert Holmes). It was the sound track when we partied "All Night Long" (Lionel Richie). It taught me that music can be both well-done and enjoyable to large audiences, which I try to remember when writing pieces in the contemporary classical mode.

So, thanks, SiriusXM, for highlighting this music. Please "Do It again" (Steely DAN). And, Lisa, "You get the best of my love" (The Eagles).

Peter and Lisa W. Altschul

PART VII

CULTURE WAR

In which I explore some of the hot button issues that divide us: family breakdown, criminal justice, abortion, climate change, trade, and health care.

LOVE IS BLIND

February 19, 2013

During the past couple of years, conservative pundits have riffed about how college graduates are far more likely to be married and financially stable than those with only a high school diploma. They encourage us college graduates to preach what we practice, and argue that the best way to lift people out of poverty is to encourage them to engage in long-term marital relationships. Intuitively, this makes sense, as a couple with a shared vision can better harness their strengths to address life's challenges than two people working alone.

But it wasn't true for me.

While growing up, I dreamed about falling in love and getting married to an intelligent, witty woman with a sexy voice, but after finishing graduate school, I left that dream behind. It seemed unreachable, and I was happy enough with the marriage between my Active Professional Life and my Quiet Social Life, made easier with the assistance of five guide dogs.

But then along came Lisa. We got engaged on my fiftieth birthday, and married six months later.

This marriage-will-make-it-easier advice doesn't seem relevant to many of my friends who have been totally blind for most of their lives and have been successful pioneers at work. We are all college graduates who lived in imperfect but good-enough homes. We have worked in organizations where we were the only employee who was blind. Each of us have struggled, made mistakes, broken our share of barriers, and have risen at least to the level of middle management.

Yet none of us have fit the marriage-for-a-lifetime paradigm; one has not yet married; three got married for the first time in our forties or fifties; and one is in his fourth marriage. I also know several totally blind couples who make less money yet are in long-term good-enough marriages.

Although my data doesn't come close to matching the rigors of a well-designed sociological study, I wonder why so many of my successful-at-work friends with college degrees who are totally blind don't fit the conservatives' prescription for success. Yes, it's harder for us to compete in the mating game because while love might be blind, the I'm-interested-in-you cues are largely visual. Yes, it's harder for us to get around, especially if we don't live in places with good mass transportation systems. And many sighted people can't quite imagine marrying a person who can't see them.

It's also true that building a trusting relationship to marriage takes time and energy, and as my mother regularly reminds me, we blind people often need more time and energy to get stuff done.

Since marrying Lisa, I have spent most of my time and energy learning how best to support her PhD quest and her efforts to raise three children, complicated by a pack of standard poodles, health issues, and a python named Monty. While I have written a memoir, composed several choral anthems, completed various consulting gigs, and continue to do volunteer work, I have not been a full-time employee, meaning I have more control of my time and energy.

But if I were to land a full-time job, Lisa and I would have to find other ways to support each other. We are fortunate, though, that we have a solid foundation from which to build.

But people near the poverty level don't have the luxury of leaving a job to nurture a mutually supportive marriage. Like my totally blind friends and me, they often must cope with unavailable, unreliable, or overcrowded public transportation to get to their job which, unlike many of our jobs, are soul-numbing, monotonous, and emotionally draining. Add to that financial and family pressures, and it's no wonder that people near the poverty level have less success with marriage — and failure breeds failure.

The marry-the-right-person and keeping-marriages-together workshops and mentoring programs that groups like *Focus on the Family* and *Family Life Today* promote might help people looking to succeed in their marriages, but they presume a preexisting interest in marriage. The attitudes and skills they are trying to communicate take time and patience to practice

— resources that are in especially short supply among people struggling to make ends meet. Moreover, these programs fail to acknowledge that too much stress too soon without balancing supports will likely condemn a marriage to failure, and less income is correlated with more stress.

So what might be done to help people with low-incomes find the time to nurture their marriages that we college graduates take for granted?

Progressives suggest an increase in the minimum wage, better mass transportation, quality healthcare, and better supports for children — programs that most conservatives oppose because of budgetary concerns and fear of an overreaching government.

Can we come together to bridge these class and philosophical divides so that more of us can benefit from the power of a long-term mutually-supportive relationship, or will people near the poverty level continue to search for other ways to find the emotional support they need?

And speaking of marriage...

Lisa, your Valentine's Day flowers are on the kitchen counter with love from your imperfect but hopefully good-enough husband.

GOOD ENOUGH

May 4, 2015

Last week, Senator and presidential candidate Rand Paul argued that "lack of fathers" was one of the root causes of the chaos Baltimore has been experiencing during the past week.

"Where are the fathers?" Lee Culpepper (1) asked in a recent column. He then rattled off some dreary statistics: eighty-five percent of the youths in prison; sixty-three percent of youth suicides; seventy percent of teenage pregnancies; eighty percent of rapists; eighty-five percent of children with behavioral problems; and seventy-one percent of high school dropouts come from homes without fathers.

These statistics mirror those I came across while working towards my master's degree in social work in the 1990s. Since then, evidence suggests that children do better with two parents in the house. So, many social conservatives argue, we can begin decreasing youth thuggery and dysfunctional behavior by decreasing welfare payments, encouraging both parents to stay together while raising their children, and allowing the church to take the government's place.

However, one of my social work professors argued that in order for kids to benefit from two-parent households, both parents needed to be good enough — not perfect, she stressed, just good enough. She later acknowledged that this term was hard to define, but that kids would probably do better if removed from parents (usually dads) who engage in incest, beat their spouses, regularly bully their children, are unrepentant substance abusers, or engage in violent crime. But conservative Christian leaders rarely address issues related to domestic violence and child abuse,

162

and when they do, they often claim that the media and big government overstate the prevalence of these phenomena to justify the need for welfare programs.

Senator Paul's lack of fathers comment also caused me to wonder about the quality of fathering received by those white male police officers who engage in thuggery against African Americans. Steve Chapman (2), in a recent column, noted that according to *The Baltimore Sun,* city officials had paid out $5.7 million since 2011 to settle 102 lawsuits alleging police abuse, including broken bones, brain injury, organ failure, and death. Yet in nearly every case, the victim was found not to have done anything legally wrong.

Might some of these officers engaging in police abuse witnessed domestic violence that their fathers committed against their wives or experienced paternal rage and/or desertion? Might it be possible that some join the police force for the same reason young African American men join gangs?

Zaid Jilani (3) reported that Senator Paul's twenty-two-year-old son crashed his car into an occupied vehicle while driving drunk — the third time that police have caught him engaging in behavior connected with drinking too much. To what degree can we be proud of a criminal justice system where a young African American male living in poverty and guilty of nothing can end up dead after interacting with a police officer while a white young male from affluent surroundings to date has experienced no legal consequences as a result of three alcohol-related infractions?

Perhaps, Senator Paul should stop making future lack of fathers remarks while continuing to push for reform of the criminal justice system. Perhaps, each of us should refrain from using words like "thuggery" unless we're willing to use such terms when describing violent acts of people in groups that we support. And let's remember that our solutions don't need to be perfect, just good enough.

(1) http://clashdaily.com/2015/04/where-are-the-fathers-heres-how-liberals-brought-on-the-living-hell-in-baltimore/

(2) http://townhall.com/columnists/stevechapman/2015/04/30/riots-in-baltimore-seen-and-unseen-n1992199

(3) http://www.alternet.org/news-amp-politics/rand-paul-blames-lack-fathers-baltimore-unrest-his-own-son-was-just-arrested-drunk

A BIAS TOWARDS SPEED

October 22, 2013

Recently, three articles have appeared on AlterNet describing how police officers assaulted three men with disabilities and/or people assisting them.

In the first, Emily Shire (1) wrote about how a young man with Down syndrome living in Frederick County, Maryland died of asphyxiation outside of a movie theater even though his aide warned them about his condition. In the second, Alex Kane (2) wrote about how four police officers in Manhattan Beach, California had "terrorized" a child with mental retardation and "brutalized" his caretaker while cracking down on gay sex in public rest rooms. in the third, Natasha Lennard (3) wrote about how, in Dallas, Texas, police officers seriously wounded a man with mental retardation even though he was standing still with his hands by his side.

These incidents reminded me of my major interaction with police officers. My guide dog, Dunbar, and I were hurrying home from Grand Central Station in New York City late one early spring night in 1995. As I approached the corner of Third Avenue and Fifty-Fourth Street, the traffic on Fifty-Fourth Street began moving, meaning that it was safe for me to cross Third Avenue, something I had done regularly since 1982.

Halfway across the street, a car knocked me down and dragged Dunbar and me for several feet before screeching to a stop. Someone identifying himself as a retired police officer assisted me to my feet and asked if I was OK. After assisting us the rest of the way across Third Avenue, he told me firmly not to move.

As Dunbar and I stood alone shivering slightly, I remember the stranger who had assisted me dashing back into the street and shouting at the driver "to stay the fuck where you are." When two police officers arrived, I remember him telling them that the light was in my favor, and that the male driver had tried to leave the scene. I remember learning that the driver was driving an expensive car and that he couldn't produce his driver's license when asked to do so. I remember the police officers not talking to me for at least twenty minutes until offering to drive Dunbar and me home.

"Will anyone be arrested?" I asked from the back of the stuffy patrol car.

"No," someone said brusquely.

"But I heard someone preventing them from leaving the scene and that the male driver didn't have his license."

"No," I was told, "a female was driving the car."

Dunbar was unhurt and unfazed, a miracle when considering that many guide dogs can no longer work after nearly getting hit by a hard-charging car. Despite a sore lower back, I was able to maintain my busy schedule. An insurance representative of the driver who hit me visited my apartment to offer me enough money to buy a new suit to replace the one that had been destroyed and to make a donation to the school that trained Dunbar.

Each incident has at least two sides. The Maryland man with Downs syndrome was acting violently outside of the movie theater. In Manhattan Beach, California, the male caretaker was assisting the disabled child to go to the bathroom. In Dallas, police had been called because the man with mental retardation had been waving a knife around. And I have often wondered if the person assisting me was really a retired police officer.

In the October 9 AlterNet article, Emily Shire (1) quoted James Mulvaney, a professor at New York's John Jay College of Criminal Justice, as saying that "law enforcement training tends to focus on the fast rather than the slow, to charge ahead rather than pull back." That's sensible: if a bad guy is assaulting me, I want that bias towards speed.

The downside, however, is that speed magnifies the power of prejudice and fear, increasing the likelihood of poor communication and accidental assaults. This reduces trust between law enforcement and people from underrepresented groups, resulting in less cooperation, fewer successfully closed criminal cases, and increased frustration among officers whose on-the-job stress levels are already too high.

The likelihood of violent acts might be reduced if more police officers with experience working with people significantly different from them are hired and promoted, as the skills and temperament gleaned from these experiences can increase effectiveness and lessen the likelihood of mistakes. Perhaps then people with developmental and intellectual disabilities (and those from other underrepresented groups) will be better served. And perhaps future officers will take us blind people more seriously when light-dependent people who drive recklessly knock us down while we're trying to cross the street.

(1) http://www.alternet.org/killed-cops-over-movie-ticket-how-police-hurt-disabled
(2) http://www.alternet.org/california-cops-trying-bust-public-gay-sex-arrested-disabled-childs-caregiver-wrongfully
(3) http://www.alternet.org/dallas-police-shoot-mentally-ill-man-standing-street

RAND PAUL'S SMOKESCREEN

April 27, 2015

Recently, Senator and presidential candidate Rand Paul posed a challenge to Debbie Wasserman Schultz, the head of the Democratic National Committee.

"You go back and you ask Debbie Wasserman Schultz if she's OK with killing a seven-pound baby that is not born yet," Senator Paul demanded when journalists pressed him for specifics about his views on abortion rights. "Ask her when life begins, and you ask Debbie when it's okay to protect life. When you get an answer from Debbie, get back to me."

My name is Peter, not Debbie, but I'm going to answer Senator Paul's question, based on my experience conducting dialogues between pro-choice and pro-life activists in the late 1990s.

"Senator Paul," pro-choice activists might say, "we don't like the idea of abortion; indeed, most of us believe that the procedure does destroy a life. While the decision to terminate a pregnancy should not be taken lightly, we believe that a woman, with guidance from her doctor and others she trusts, should make this decision without government interference."

While talking about abortion rights with pro-choice women, I have been struck by how many have said that while they supported a woman's right to choose, they didn't think they could go through with an abortion themselves. I have also heard about women identifying themselves as pro-life having an abortion to shield themselves from parental fury.

The abortion issue's main fault line is not the degree to which activists on both sides of the issue believe that abortion is moral, but the role government should play. While most people agree that the government shouldn't force a woman to have an abortion against her will, consider the following questions:

1. To what extent should government bureaucrats fund and regulate clinics that provide abortions and centers that discourage abortions?
2. When should the person who has had an abortion be allowed to deduct the costs as a medical expense on her tax return?
3. To what extent should Medicaid and other programs fund contraceptives?
4. Given that abortion rates go up when economic conditions worsen, what government policies should be implemented to buffer people from a dysfunctional economy?
5. Since many people have abortions because of the fear of giving birth to a child with a significant disability, how, if at all, should government bureaucracies support parents who have children with disabilities?

    And to me, the most vexing question:

6. If abortion becomes illegal, with what should the government charge a woman who has had an abortion?

If we really believe abortion is murdering an unborn baby, then shouldn't she be charged with murder? Certainly, sex partners, parents, and others often pressure — even force — women to have abortions, but how is that different from somebody who murders someone while robbing a bank because they need money to feed an out-of-control drug addiction?

While talking to people about my work with pro-life and pro-choice activists, I often say that male activists on both sides of the issue have been the biggest barrier in preventing some sort of compromise that everyone could live with.

"I know this is impossible," I add, "but if we shielded women activists from male activists and provided them with privacy and quality support in working through the issues, I think something transformative might happen."

In the meantime, we could encourage more productive conversations if we stop shouting at each other about how much we hate women and babies and think through ways that the government could play a more effective role in promoting both life and choice. And Senator Paul, instead of setting up a smokescreen, why don't you talk about your take on the role government should play concerning abortion, and then invite Ms. Wasserman Schultz to do the same?

INVASION OF THE RED HERRING

February 5, 2015

The anti-global warming crowd won at least a short-term public relations victory by voting for a Senate resolution supporting the existence of global warming.

"See," they seemed to be saying, "we can be reasonable."

They then opposed another Senate resolution indicating that human actions were a major contributor to global warming.

"Not only are we reasonable, we're pragmatic," they seemed to be saying with this second vote. "If we humans didn't cause the problem, then we aren't responsible for addressing it."

Really?

Imagine if more and more people began to be covered in red slime that smelled like rotten herring, as well as causing a significant portion of the population to become partially blind and/or deaf. Media figures would interview some of the victims, speculate on the cause, provide guidance on how we can protect ourselves, and highlight the human suffering in tones ranging from somber to cheerful. Over time, more and more astronomers, astrophysicists, and biologists would identify the source: a herring-shaped comet that was racing towards us.

"It might or might not collide with Earth," a spokesperson for the coalition of scientists exploring the phenomenon tell an interviewer on Vixen News, "but we must find ways to mitigate the suffering, and develop strategies to divert this invader."

"But," the interviewer splutters, "we should do nothing, as humans didn't cause this."

Really?

I'm not interested in heading towards a dusty, dreary, and decaying earth as described in the film *Interstellar*. Now that almost all of us agree that global warming is real, shouldn't we start working together to mitigate the consequences and develop strategies to head off potentially far more disastrous effects despite our disagreements about the extent to which we humans contribute to the problem? After all, pillaging for profit can only get us so far.

And beware of the red herring.

TRADE TRIALS

April 14, 2016

"What's good for GM is good for the country."

Growing up, that mantra served as the starting point for most political discussions, and remained constant throughout the 1980s and 1990s. Then NAFTA, the first major trade deal, sailed through Congress. Other trade deals followed.

But towards the end of the old millennium, technology disruptions, the harsh consequences of corporate relocations and prior trade agreements, the repeal of legislation passed during the Great Depression, increased income inequality, and widely-publicized ethically-challenged actions of business leaders caused more and more people to question the quality of the relationship between big business and the rest of us.

The current over-the-top performance of our presidential campaign circus masks the divide between those who believe that big business, with government support, is good for the country and those that believe that big business's power needs to be reigned in. This fault line cuts through both major parties, and explains the sharp disagreements concerning the most recent trade deal: the not-yet-ratified Trans-Pacific Partnership (TPP) agreement.

"Trade benefits America!" supporters trumpet.

"We agree," respond opponents in more muted tones.

"Over-all, good well-paying jobs have increased as a result of prior trade agreements."

"Show us these jobs," opponents insist.

"And even if no new jobs are created, countries that sell us their products invest their gains here, making it easier for businesses to expand."

"But why would businesses want to expand if they don't have enough customers?"

"Trade agreements allow low-income people to buy stuff more cheaply," supporters say.

"If they have any money to spend."

"Trade agreements foster healthy competition."

"No, they make it easier for big businesses to engage in corruption, hide profits, and conceal their dirty deeds."

And around and around it goes.

Like other agreements, the TPP is only as effective as those who regulate it want it to be, and given increasingly close ties among businesses and governments, environmental and labor protections in the treaty are not likely to be enforced.

And what about that portion that allows big businesses and foreign investors to sue a government whose laws cut into their profits?

"Sorry," I can hear a politician saying at a press conference, his voice oozing with earnestness, "but I can't support a policy addressing climate change because it's just too expensive."

Wink, wink; nod, nod.

It's hard to disentangle the effects of trade policy from other factors that have caused increased job instability and income inequality. Paul Krugman (1) recently wrote that "agreements that lead to more trade neither create nor destroy jobs."

But perhaps we can come together to, as Warren Buffett (2) suggests, build shock absorbers that protect people from economic earthquakes while reconnecting big business with the best interest of the rest of us.

Or we could use the Donald Trump approach.

"Build a wall! You're fired!"

Afterword

We chose the latter option. Sad.

(1) https://www.nytimes.com/2016/03/11/opinion/trade-and-tribulation.html?_r=0
(2) http://www.strategy-business.com/blog/Buffett-s-Warning-on-Economic-Gloom?gko=5a4ad

SMALLBALL HEALTH CARE

June 4, 2017

"Na na na na, na na na na, hey hey hey, goodbye."

Thus chorused some Congressional Democrats after the American Health Care Act (AHCA) narrowly passed the House of Representatives.

Another disconnect between the high and mighty and the rest of us, for this "Na Na na" chant became irrelevant at least ten years ago, and back then, it was used only when victory was assured.

Sad.

Shortly afterwards, a group of old white male Republican Congress members joined with President Trump and others to celebrate on the White House lawn with beer and cigars.

Like a bunch of clueless frat brats.

Pathetic.

Politicians also seem to have forgotten one of the reasons Donald Trump was elected president: the disgust with, and mistrust of, the interconnected matrix of big business, big government, big military, and big religion. Instead of seeking ways to save money while improving healthcare, the AHCA has the feel of determining the size of the deckchairs that big healthcare insurers, big hospitals, bigshot medical practitioners, mammoth drug companies, large employers, and big government bureaucrats will luxuriate on as the Healthcare Titanic cruises on calm seas. As Hal Scherz (1) puts it:

"The real problem is that not a single replacement plan for Obamacare ... addresses the true cost of health care, which is obscene."

During the past several months, I have come across several

recommendations from Hal Scherz (1), Michael Hamilton (2), Senator Ted Cruz (3), and others (4) (5) that might lower costs while improving the patient experience by rejiggering the power differential among matrix members. These recommendations include:

* Simplifying the drug approval process a la Europe and Canada, and allowing patients to import medicine from these countries.
* Allowing people to maintain their health plan between and among jobs.
* Encouraging small businesses to band together to get better rates for their employees.
* Continuing to incorporate telemedicine and other technologies into the doctor-patient relationship.
* Making it easier for physician assistants, nurse practitioners, dental therapists, and midwives to play a greater role in patient care.
* Piloting programs where doctors provide patients a range of preventive care services and basic tests for a monthly fee.
* Reducing barriers to allow other organizations to compete with hospitals.
* Publicizing successes in Colorado, Rhode Island, and other states that show promise in reducing health care challenges while saving money.

The biggest bridge separating progressives and conservatives is the role the federal government should play.

"Universal health care!" progressives proclaim.

Not sellable in our culture of rugged individualism.

"Get the feds out of the healthcare business!" chorus conservatives.

Unrealistic, for at minimum, the federal government needs healthy young people to serve in the military in order to defend the United States and make it more difficult for plagues to cross state lines so that commerce can continue to flow.

More and more successful businesses are giving more responsibility to those closer to the customer after giving them clear goals, guidance, and resources. Devolving responsibility to states a la these successful businesses makes good sense if we as a people developed clear goals that each state would work towards meeting.

But what should the federal government do if a state spectacularly fails to reach one of these goals, especially if this failure endangers those living in adjacent states? Business leaders can fire incompetent employees, but we can't say "you're fired" to a failing state.

Perhaps, a bill offered by Senators Bill Cassidy (R-LA) and Susan Collins (R-ME) would be a good starting point to give each state more responsibility. This bill allows state governments to decide whether to stick with the Affordable Care Act (ACA) or use ninety-five percent of the money they would receive under the ACA to try something different. Let's begin experimenting and publicize successes.

Or we could continue building those unhealthy walls between us.

(1) https://townhall.com/columnists/halscherz/2017/02/21/letter-to-president-trump-you-have-missed-the-best-resource-in-fixing-health-carebig-time-n2288350
(2) https://townhall.com/columnists/michaelhamilton/2017/02/16/show-constituents-love-by-giving-health-care-freedom-n2286508
(3) http://www.politico.com/magazine/story/2017/03/ted-cruz-obamacare-repeal-214854
(4) http://www.alternet.org/personal-health/family-planning-miracle-colorado-program-has-teen-births-and-abortions-drop-half-and
(5) https://townhall.com/columnists/stephenmoore/2017/04/04/what-congress-can-learn-from-the-rhode-island-miracle-n2308145

PART VIII

POTUS POLITICS

Where I harumph about presidential politics and leadership from the perspective of one grouchy human and two ornery service dogs.

FEELINGS TRUMP THOUGHTS

March 9, 2016

"There are many things I don't quite get about this election year," I said while munching on a piece of cake in honor of the birthday of my church choir's conductor, "but the thing I find most weird is how conservative Christians are supporting Trump over one of their own."

"Trump is more of an outsider," someone suggested.

"But none of the Republican elite like Cruz."

"But he is still a senator."

"And Trump has political connections through his businesses."

Three days later, I witnessed the most bizarre political theater I have ever seen.

I missed Act One, when former Governor Mitt Romney trashed The Donald in front of an adoring audience.

"He's not smart!" ... "He's a terrible businessman!" ... "He's not a conservative!" ... "He's a fraud!" Governor Romney proclaimed.

I tuned into Act Two, where a chorus of talking heads gushed about Romney's calling out of Trump and wondering if his soliloquy would derail The Donald? Shouldn't he have said this earlier? Won't this speech, coming from the consummate insider, strengthen the resolve of Trump supporters?

Then came Act Three, Trump's responding soliloquy, in front of a throng of admiring fans.

I sat spellbound on my couch with my guide dog lying next to me as businessman Trump spoke about Romney's ineptness as a candidate; how Romney stabbed him in the back after begging him for his support;

and how he had hosted two fund-raisers for Romney that required him to replace the carpet because of the mud Romney supporters had brought in due to a driving rain outside.

"Maybe I should ask him to reimburse me for the cost of replacing the carpet," The Donald suggested. His fans laughed and cheered.

Mr. Trump spent the balance of his speech trumpeting his negotiating skills and his success as a businessman.

But this political play was far from over. During Act Four, the Talking Heads Chorus gushed about Trump's speech and wondered how the action thus far would affect that night's debate.

I missed Act Five, The Debate, but rejoined the audience in Act Six, The Post-Debate Show, during which I learned all about the connection between the size of male hands and the size of our penises.

After several days of contemplative, cleansing meditation, I think I understand better the disconnect between Senator Cruz and the conservative Christian tribe. Ted talks Christian thoughts, and revels in the contempt that others feel towards him. "I'm smarter than everyone else, and have unshakable values," he thunders. "So vote for me!"

Meanwhile, Donald Trump engaged his listeners' empathy while sharing stories about his relationship with Mr. Romney, as all of us have experienced the betrayals, the stabs in the back, the stupidity of others who refuse to recognize our strengths, and generally being dissed. "I get where you're coming from," he seems to be saying, "and I'll have your backs as I use my considerable business skills to make America great again!"

What about the Senator Rubio-businessman Trump penis size tussle?

Penis size signifies virility and strength — the strength to subdue those foreign and domestic enemies that beset Mr. Trump's primarily white male audience with an authoritarian streak: upity women, upity blacks, Mexican thugs, and Muslims, amongst others.

Like President Reagan, Donald Trump connects with his audience through images and stories. He understands the value of optimism and flexibility. As for unshakable values, not!

Most of all, The Donald understands that feelings trump thoughts.

DOG DAYS

August 21, 2016

"Labrador love! Labrador love! Labrador love!" chanted a crowd of Labradors of all sizes and hues at the Labrador convention of the Service Dogs of America. The chanting continued, with joyous panting, tail-waggings, and leaping about as their presidential candidate, a stocky middle-aged black Lab named Snuffles approached the podium.

"I humbly accept your nomination as the presidential candidate of the Labrador Party," Snuffles said, tail wagging gently. "A true honor."

More cheering and chanting.

"We Labradors are the backbone of the service dog community," Snuffles continued. "We work hard, but we love to play. And eat."

A volley of laughing barks.

"But, most importantly, we love. We love each other. We love humans. We love our enemies!"

"Seriously?" snorted Hunter, an eighty-pound multicolored standard poodle with the soul of a comedian. He raised his head from the couch he was occupying in the living room of a large house many miles from the convention chaos.

"But we do love everyone!" said Heath from another couch in the same living room. Heath was a guide dog with the soul of a football player. "It's one of the main reasons we Labs are so good at begging for food."

"But loving your enemies?" Hunter grunted. "I know that Jesus human told humans to love their enemies, but—"

"However," Snuffles continued, his voice slightly raised. "There's a time for honesty. So, I must seriously ask: how can our opponents have chosen a poodle named Fluffy as their nominee for president?"

Howls of mirth.

"I mean," continued Snuffles, "we know all about poodles' insistence that they get their own way. And they're snobs, prancing about with their heads in the air."

More howls from the conventioneers.

"But we want to be the poodle party, like we were 150 years ago. Isn't it time that you poodles try something new? Vote for us, and in four years, ninety-five percent of you will vote for us."

"Labrador love!" cascaded through the hall.

"Poodle pride! Poodle pride! Poodle pride!" chanted a crowd of standard poodles of all sizes and hues at the poodle convention of the Service Dogs of America. The chanting continued, with joyous panting, tail-twitchings, and leaping about as their presidential candidate, a tall, youthful black standard poodle approached the podium.

"My name is Fluffy!" he boomed, tail twitching. "And I proudly accept your nomination as presidential candidate of the Poodle Party."

Poodles cheered, prancing in the aisles.

"Sure, we're new to the service dog scene," he continued. "But we're making great strides! We're smarter and more motivated than those lazy Labradors."

"Lazy?" Heath asked, spread out on a king-sized bed.

"And of course our heads are in the air," Fluffy continued. "We can see what's happening around us far more than those Labradors who have their noses to the ground. We're poodles; we're the best; and we know it!" Fluffy thundered.

"Poodle pride! Poodle pride!" Poodle pride!"

"And how can those Labradors pretend to love everything and not call the problem for what it is!" Fluffy howled. "Radical human terrorists!"

"Honestly!" Heath growled, springing off of the bed and snatching a sock from the floor.

"But abusive humans do exist!" Hunter growled, grabbing the other end of the sock.

"Love your enemies!" Heath taunted, the sock in his mouth muffling his words.

"Not that again!" Hunter growled from the other end of the sock. "Everyone knows we're smarter, more agile, more alert."

"You poodles are too smart for your own good," Heath countered, shaking his head from side to side. "You're just too doggone antisocial."

"Well, one thing's for sure," Hunter said. "You're not a coward like Snuffles."

"What?" Heath asked, accidentally letting go of the sock.

"You criticized my breed face to face, not in front of a crowd of cultish fans."

"Fluffy did the same thing," Heath pointed out. "I wonder what they're protecting."

"Their egos?" Hunter pondered, standing still, head in the air, the sock still dangling from his mouth.

"Perhaps we could challenge Snuffles and Fluffy to make their remarks away from their followers," Heath suggested, his nose to the floor.

"No, they're both cowards," Hunter grunted. "But we could do it."

"What?" Heath asked, alert.

"We could talk about our lives together," Hunter said, a gleam in his eye. "How we've learned to work as a team to manipulate our humans."

So Hunter, using his comedic genius, had Labradors howling in the aisle as he described how he opens the refrigerator door so that Heath can grab choice bits of food; how they run with glee to another room; and devour their plunder, leaving shreds of package for humans to clean up.

Heath, harnessing his football smarts, talked about how it was OK to be with your own kind, but that teamwork could do far more than working alone.

"We can win the game against humans with much less effort," Heath said, his voice raw with emotion, "when we work together."

"Woof, WOOF!" barked the poodles.

And when the election came around, a coalition of Labradors and poodles elected Ace, an elderly, dignified golden retriever, as president.

DONALD TRUMPS RUSH

July 25, 2016

Whenever I hear Donald Trump speak, I think of Rush Limbaugh.

Between 1988 and 1998, I listened to Rush at least twice a week while working on projects related to my education and employment. At first, a good deal of his commentary seemed over the top, but I found myself laughing in spite of myself. During his earlier years, he balanced his snarky comments about others with a willingness to poke fun at himself.

After Bill Clinton was elected president, Rush seemed to become angrier, less self-aware, and more predictable. He spent less time criticizing ideas and more time trashing the character of the people who disagreed with him.

If his victims weren't white non-disabled straight males, he used those differences as part of his belittling campaigns. Women who disagreed with him were either ugly, lesbian, whores, or feminazis. "We love you!" Rush chanted in a poor imitation of Nelson Mandela's voice during Mr. Mandela's first tour of the United States. His attacks on Hillary Clinton were especially vicious. His messages were clear: if you don't agree with me, you're stupid, a jerk, or both; I don't apologize because I'm rarely wrong; and we white straight nondisabled men are the true victims.

Rush became more and more popular and influential among conservatives. Once while in a hotel room in State College, Pennsylvania in 1995, I found his resonant, pompous voice on three of the four AM stations I could access. Conservative Christians and their Republican leaders revered him, refusing to criticize any of his patter. But by the time I moved to Washington, Dc in 1998, Rush and his acolytes had stopped my slide towards conservatism, and I found other sources of entertainment between noon and three PM on weekdays.

Like Rush, Donald Trump is a consummate communicator and salesperson. Like Rush, his primary fans are white males. Like Rush, he is more interested in trashing the character of those who disagree with him than discussing solutions to the problems we face. Like Rush, he will incorporate differences into his attacks, as Megyn Kelly and his two prior wives have discovered.

Woe to those who challenge The Donald. He continues to trash those he defeated in the Republican primary, and has bombarded small businesses who claim he owes them money with blizzards of lawsuits to stop them from pressing their claims in court.

Both Rush Limbaugh and Donald Trump have played a key role in unifying the conservative Christian, neoconservative, and libertarian wings of the Republican party, not by finding common ground on their policy differences, but by establishing who's in and who's out and by crafting the crash-and-burn rhetorical approach to demean those outside of the GOP's orbit. While presidents George H. W. Bush and George W. Bush; governors Jeb Bush and John Kasich; senator John McCain; and others haven't bowed to The Donald's will, their refusal to strongly criticize Rush Limbaugh's more incendiary comments have given them less credibility.

We'll never know if Mr. Trump's candidacy could have been nipped in the bud if these leaders had stood up to Rush's bullying behavior, but we do know that all of us are stuck with him until at least November eighth.

Or perhaps until the end of January, 2025.

TRAILBLAZING TRIALS

August 1, 2016

Murderer! Marie Antoinette! Tear-faker! Adulterer! Liar! Hellary! Lesbian! Frigid! Crooked! Witch! Lucifer's embassador!

Some of the names the Hillary-haters have used during their twenty-five year campaign against Hillary Clinton. To them, she's the boogeybitch, the icon of everything that's wrong with the universe.

Now she's the Democratic party's nominee for president of the United States.

Hillary's gutsy. Smart. Experienced. Cool under pressure. Policy wonk.

Then, there's Whitewater. The State Department e-mail mess. Her support of the invasions of Iraq and Libya. Her failed efforts to reform healthcare.

It's hard to assess Hillary Clinton's qualifications because of the unrelenting artillery barrage surrounding her. Her allies seem more interested in trashing Trump instead of highlighting her accomplishments.

Then, there's the first factor: the first woman to be one step away from becoming president. How much of the controversy surrounding her involves her role as a woman trail blazer? To what degree would the uproar over her actions be as intense if she was a man? And how to factor in the current political polarization?

Trailblazing is tough, requiring a combination of contradictory characteristics: soft sturdiness; flexible firmness; and shrewd gentleness. We pioneers have less control of our personal brands. We sometimes spectacularly succeed, but fall short more often. And our failures often make it harder for those who want to follow our paths.

After moving to Columbia, Missouri, to deepen my relationship with my future wife, I started applying for management positions at one of the largest employers in the area. Every couple of months during the next two years, I interviewed for a variety of positions with my guide dog by my side. Ultimately, a work team hired me to assist them to address conflicts they were experiencing.

Shortly after beginning this assignment, a visually-impaired employee of this organization was laid off, and I mentioned my conflict management work in a cover letter to a recently-hired senior leader. Soon, complete strangers identifying themselves as organization employees began asking me about what caused the lay-off of the other blind person, making me wonder how such news traveled so fast throughout the organization and the extent to which a lay-off of a non-disabled person would generate such interest. At around the same time, the head of the business unit I was working with called to tell me that my services were no longer needed, as there had never been a conflict within their unit. Since then, all future job applications to this organization have resulted in deafening nonresponses.

Surely Senator Clinton must be aware of the challenges of being the first. Why then did she make speeches to financial institutions for lavish fees when most of us thought she would run for president? She didn't need the money, and coddling investment firm leaders is politically toxic.

And why, as secretary of state, use a private server to do government business? Sure, her male predecessors did something similar, but they weren't running for president. The ultimate outcry was predictable and painful to watch. So were the lies she told.

It appears that my lapse in judgment and the failings of my visually-impaired peer have severed my relationship with that local employer. Mrs. Clinton's strengths, coupled with Donald Trump's over-the-top nastiness, the overreach of her opponents, and President Obama's popularity, might allow her to reach her goal despite her judgment lapses. But if she fails, other women with presidential ambitions might have to wait a while.

I'm rooting for Hillary. We trailblazers need to stick together.

SIZE MATTERS

January 28, 2017

Why did Donald Trump win the presidential election? Why was voter turn-out so low?

Disgust with Senator Hillary Clinton? Check. Irritation with DC gridlock? Check. Gender and race bias? Check. General unease about the direction in which the United States is heading? Check.

But the main reason, I believe, is that most of us fear and loath big bureaucracies.

The Tea Party's primary energy source was the overreaching federal bureaucracy, while Occupy Wall Street focused its wrath on the big banks, military contractors, oil conglomerates, and other large private sector bureaucracies that have become too big to fail. Almost every politician and talking head has complained about how the big government and big business bureaucracies are in bed with each other with the lights down low to give birth to offspring that benefit the big people while diminishing the rest of us. The Trump campaign did a much better job connecting with this anti-bureaucratic bias.

Conditions on the ground are causing big bureaucracies to worry. Columnists from all over the political spectrum have argued that setting clear goals, being agile, using technology wisely, and learning from mistakes separate effective from ineffective organizations. Technology appears to be moving us away from lumbering organizations where employees march in lockstep towards more agile groups that practice guerrilla warfare, guerrilla marketing, and improvisation.

But change is hard, and the Big Government Big Business Bureaucratic

Alliance (BGBBBA) has banded together behind the scenes to write regulations, raise money, develop marketing campaigns, and make it more difficult for others to compete. After all, it's much more fun to make love, not war, while expanding perks and maintaining the status quo.

Big bureaucracies can be beautiful if they use their size advantage to create something valuable instead of just enriching their friends and shareholders. Small bureaucracies can be ugly if political infighting and poor planning prevent them from using their smallness to their advantage. Big government can be beautiful if it sets high expectations and shares best practices without overly engaging in how things get done.

Davids of the world, unite! A few well-aimed stones can perform miracles.

THE SHAGGY DOG PARTNERSHIP

November 13, 2016

"Those humans are barking up the wrong tree," declared Hunter, a multicolored standard poodle. He and his partner, Heath, a black Labrador guide dog, had just inhaled the contents of a full box of Lucky Charms and a large piece of Brie cheese.

Heath belched loudly, looking for more crumbs.

"They're all growling about their election of a president," Hunter continued. "Everybody seems to hate the two leading candidates, and now that the election is over, both factions are hiding from each other."

Heath yawned.

"They should have learned from our elections. I mean both of the leading candidates for president of Service Dogs of America were pathetic," Hunter continued.

"Take Fluffy, the standard poodle candidate," Heath grunted. "The name was bad enough, but his 'service' involved guarding a precious object."

Hunter hung his head.

"I know, I know," he said. "And then he fell asleep when two different people on the same night tried to steal the object."

"The rumor is that he was stoned," Heath said, leaping onto his couch.

"And others believed that a magic harp and flute put him to sleep," Hunter said, leaping onto his couch.

Heath yawned.

"Then there's the rumor that he once had three heads," Hunter growled.

"A nasty piece of doggerel, no doubt," heath said.

Hunter leapt off of his couch. "And what about the Labrador candidate, Snuffles?"

Heath sighed deeply.

"Whenever he said 'seriously', everyone howled with glee. I never got the joke."

"And he apparently murdered a human," Hunter continued, his head in the air.

"Trumped-up charges!" Heath barked.

"Then there's the rumor that he was a human in dog's clothing."

"Ridiculous; the things that some hounds believe," Heath said, slithering from his couch.

"The important thing, though," Hunter said, "is that we persuaded the pack that we could do better than a poodle who sleeps on the job and a Labrador who might not even be a dog."

Heath padded to one of the three water bowls scattered throughout the house. "And all we really did was to tell stories and encourage others to share stories of their own."

"Heroic stories," Hunter said, prancing about. "Funny stories. Sad stories. Inspiring stories."

"And through these stories," Heath called between slurps of water, "we realized we could forge a partnership between Labrador love and poodle pride to find better candidates."

Hunter smiled. "And now we're being paid to continue our work with service dogs. It's so nice to be eating from the government bowl."

"If only humans could remember the power of storytelling to bring people together," Heath said, belching loudly. "They would be much happier."

"You do remember one of our new president's more annoying sayings?" Hunter asked, heading towards the doggy door.

Heath joined him there. "Which one?"

"To err is human, to forgive is canine!"

Both dogs hurried outside, leaving behind an aura of sugary cereal and sour cheese.

Top dogs and co-founders The Shaggy Dog Partnership, LLC

POTUS FOR AN HOUR

January 5, 2017

The day after Donald Trump was promoted to President-Elect of the United States, I took part in an hour-long podcast during which the host asked me a variety of quirky questions. I did pretty well until he asked:

"What is the first thing you would do if you ruled the world?"

After some stuttering starts, I mumbled something about doing lots of listening.

I later remembered that most high-level leaders set boundaries to structure their listening through what they do and say; indeed, that's one of the purposes of a president's inaugural address.

So if I were in President-Elect Trump's shoes, my inaugural speech might go something like this:

"Fellow citizens:

"It is both an honor and a bit intimidating to begin my journey as your leader. While I won the election, I know that I lost the general election by the biggest margin in history. I understand that some of you have committed to do everything you can to prevent me from being successful.

"I do hope that we can continue to work towards policies on which most of us agree: reforming the criminal justice and healthcare systems, as well as the business tax code, to promote fairness, effectiveness, and efficiency. We need to come together to find a way to address a dangerously unstable world.

"I understand that the Executive branch has become too powerful, and look forward to transferring some of that power back to where it belongs: the legislative branch. But only if Congressional leaders replace their cynical cowardice with collaboration and a can-do spirit.

"However, the primary concern that unites us is the sense that the big government-big business-big military-big religion matrix has become way too powerful. We can begin addressing this by simplifying the tax code while eliminating the slew of deductions, government giveaways, and backroom deals that this matrix has come to expect. We should support small businesses to thrive, as they are the main source of job creation and innovation.

"More importantly, we should do a better job of giving more power to state and local governments after giving them clear goals to which they will be held responsible.

"Of course, there are limitations. The federal government has a constitutional obligation to create a level playing field for everyone, especially for businesses and those from underrepresented groups.

"Giving more power to the states can be problematic.

"Suppose a close friend with a disability faces constant discrimination, and the state isn't willing to take action?

"Or suppose you are pro-life and live in a state where abortion is difficult to obtain, and a clinic from a state where abortions are easier to get floods your media with ads encouraging women to visit this out-of-state clinic?

"Or suppose pollution caused in part because of a state's unwillingness to address the problem affects those living in other states?

"Or suppose citizens from a given state suffer significantly because of irresponsible actions of local government officials?

"How should the federal government respond in each of these situations?

"Yet pushing power downward seems crucial, even inevitable. More and more businesses are removing bureaucratic layers with generally positive results.

"we're no longer in the 1990s where people could live quite comfortably without turning on a computer. Now, cloud computers and the networks they spawn, 3D printers, apps, self-driving cars, and other high-tech gadgets are revolutionizing the way we live our lives — eliminating jobs while creating others -- while making products and services more affordable.

"Agility is key to addressing the challenges of this new age, and local governments have a better shot of moving more quickly to realign programs to support each of us to adjust to these turbulent times. How do we educate our kids? How do we jigger government programs to a future where jobs might be scarcer and require new skills? How do these technologies change healthcare, transportation, and the military? How do we regulate this human-technology meld in ways that benefit the most people while not submerging our humanity to computers that, through algorithms, can perform ever-more complicated tasks?

"We can start by remembering that computers cannot love.

"And what is love?

"To quote a Shaker song:

"'Love is little, love is low;

Love will make our spirits grow.

Grow in peace, grow in light;

Love will do the thing that's right.'

"That's what makes us human.

"So let our love shine forth as we, with the help of our Creator, strive to make America more magnificent.

"Thanks for listening.

Now I resign."

NEW SWAMP CREATURE DISCOVERED

April 5, 2017

Mudville, The Swamp -- Vixen News reports that zoologists claim to have discovered a new swamp-dwelling creature that they have called the trumputin.

"Everybody agrees on the existence of the trumpitus," zoologist Karen Quicksand stated. "It's classified as Donaldissimus Trumpitus, and it's best known for building complex structures that destroy everything around them. It rules a powerful land from sea to shining sea."

"And everybody agrees on the existence of the Vladimirium Putinum," Ms. Quicksand continued. "More commonly known as the putinum, it has a long history of slashing and poisoning its enemies while sowing discord among wildlife around it. It rules a larger, less powerful kingdom."

"But profound disagreement exists concerning whether these beasts mated to form the trumputin," zoologist Barney Bog explained. "On one hand, the trumputin shares traits of both the trumpitus and the putinum. A love of power that comes from being feared. A knack for destroying everything around them. A lust for more and more power."

"But Buddy Brackish is the only one who claims to have seen the trumputin in its habitat — before dying mysteriously," Mr. Bog continued. "And the only image available is murky, provoking charges that the image is fake."

This announcement provoked disbelieving snorts, fearful grunts, and joyous roars among members of the wildlife community.

"The trumputin doesn't exist," scoffed Devin Tadpole. "It's just an excuse for scientists to run from their claims of global warming. Or climate change. Or whatever the PC term is for the phenomenon that doesn't exist. We should continue to investigate how their treachery nearly cost the life of the noble trumpitus."

"We're not sure that the trumputin truly exists," explained Rachel Mudpuddle, her voice quavering slightly. "But we need to investigate to determine its whereabouts, and to figure out what we can do to defend ourselves from this poisonous force."

"Great news!" wrote columnist Pat Pawprint. "The trumputin may or may not exist, but we should do all we can to encourage it to flourish. It will knit together our two kingdoms, destroy the elites, and bring about world peace!"

Everyone interviewed for this story did agree on one thing.

All the world's a swamp.

AN EERIE SYMMETRY

August 18, 2014

In January, 2001, George W. Bush was sworn in as president of the United States, and after the September 11 terrorist attacks in New York City and northern Virginia, the world was behind him. But during the run-up to the mid-term elections of 2006, a pack of hyenas began calling him names, rejoicing in his failures, and howling about impeachment.

In January, 2009, Barack Hussein Obama was sworn in as president, and on October fifth of that year, won the Nobel Peace Prize, based on speeches he had made about the religion of Islam, nuclear proliferation, and climate change. But during the run-up to the mid-term elections of 2014, a different pack of hyenas began calling him names, rejoicing in his failures, and howling about impeachment.

One of the accusations opponents of both presidents have used is that they took (or take) too many vacations. "President Bush has taken more vacations than any other president," progressives proclaimed. "President Obama vacations as the world burns," conservatives trumpet.

This charge is so twentieth century, as the rapid advances of technology make it possible for presidents — and many of us — to stay connected with information important to us. Presidents and their staffs have the resources they need to make necessary decisions regardless of their location. This doesn't mean that the White House isn't an important place for ceremonial occasions, meetings, and for the symbolic value it has for all Americans. Suggesting, however, that only presidential work takes place there is misleading and hypocritical, since many making these pronouncements take vacations at the same time as the presidents they mock.

What would happen if the two presidents met behind closed doors to compare notes once Barack Obama's second term ends?

Perhaps, they'd commiserate about some of their opponents whose main aim was to prevent them from succeeding. Perhaps, they would comment on how much easier it is to tear down instead of building up. They might share regrets about some of the decisions they made that gave the hyenas so much ammunition. They might reflect on ways they could have used their early popularity more wisely. They might explore the value of underpromising and overdelivering.

They might also promote the benefits of telecommuting, a process they both benefitted from as president. They could talk about how telecommuting saves money and time, reduces pollution, and allows employees to gain more control over their lives — while often increasing productivity and profits.

People might counter that telecommuting reduces the quality of office relationships; that some jobs can't be done from home; and that not everyone can handle the responsibility of getting the job done away from the office.

"True," the presidents might respond, "so each organization needs to find the right balance between people working on — and off-site."

While they're at it, perhaps Presidents Bush and Obama might also promote the value of vacations to managers and workers at all income levels.

Afterword

I hope Presidents Bush and Obama will have that meeting behind closed doors.

And predictably, the anti-Trump hyenas are howling about President Trump's excessive vacation time while his supporters are praising his willingness to work away from the swamp.

ANOTHER ARMCHAIR DIAGNOSIS

May 24, 2017

Paranoia. Alzheimer's. Narcissistic Personality Disorder. Dementia.

Professional psychiatrists have diagnosed President Trump with these and other conditions without seeing him professionally.

Unethical!

I think President Trump is, to use the language of my stepkids, a creeper. A serial sexual assaulter of women. A rich brat screwing contractors and customers. A cowardly bully using swamp rules and other people to do his dirty work. A con artist obsessed with popularity and power.

And I wonder if he might have an undisclosed or undiagnosed disability.

Many talking heads have snarked about President Trump's impulsivity; his unwillingness to sit through briefings; and his refusal to read important documents -- all possible symptoms of Attention Deficit Hyperactivity Disorder or some sort of learning disability.

But even if these diagnoses are wrong, might it be possible that President Trump learns best by listening? After all, he seems to pay attention to TV news, and has changed his mind on Taiwan and NATO after talking with leaders from China and Germany.

So why isn't President Trump's inner circle playing to his strength of being able to learn through sound? Why aren't they conveying the information they think he needs to have audibly? If they can't do so in person, why don't they use available technology to convert the written word into speech?

While disability doesn't excuse despicable behavior, shouldn't progressives, with our concern for diversity and tolerance, be advocating that President Trump have the supports (or accommodations in Americans with Disabilities Act speak) that might make him more effective? And shouldn't Trump's inner circle implement these changes before whining off the record about their boss's stupidity?

More recently, talking heads have snarked about how NATO officials are encouraging heads of state to limit presentations to two to four minutes to address President Trump's ... Disability? Quirk? Whatever.

NATO summits are organized to allow participants to exchange information, develop relationships, and set goals. Most of us have attended conferences with similar aims that have fallen flat because certain participants have droned on for too long about something forgettable while others yawn, drink coffee, check their e-mail, read a book, or leave the room. Encouraging presenters to keep their remarks under four minutes sounds sensible, not only because most of us can only concentrate fully on one person's comments for no more than thirty seconds, but also because these get-togethers hinge on participants becoming actively engaged.

And pretending to listen to speeches doesn't encourage active engagement.

Didn't many of us vote against NATO's snobby rigidity? Couldn't NATO meeting planners signal that they were incorporating best practices into their design instead of complaining about having to do things differently? And shouldn't we all entertain the possibility that accommodating the needs of others might make things better for all of us?

PENCE FOR PRESIDENT!

July 20, 2018

Since President Clinton refused to resign after his sexual escapades with Monica Lewinsky were exposed, politicians from both parties have increasingly resorted to playground tactics. Throwing temper tantrums. Bullying and lying. Changing the rules in the middle of the game. Trashing others while claiming the victimhood mantle. Excusing their behavior because "They do it too," and: "It's not illegal." Donald Trump built upon these tactics to become president of the United States.

Now Republican leaders have near total control of the political seesaw, but President Trump is standing, feet firmly planted, in the way, whining about fake news and calling Republicans dopes for not passing a bill to repeal and replace the Affordable Care Act. Republicans need to put him in a permanent time-out; only they can do it.

Lying, backstabbing, and a bias towards authoritarianism are commonplace in the political playground, and while reprehensible, cannot serve as a basis for impeachment. But what about firing an FBI director to slow down the investigation into the Trump administration's Russia connection? Obstruction of justice?

Anyone listening to New York City white male conservative radio in the 1980s and 1990s would have heard about Donald Trump's connections with Italian and Russian organized crime bosses. As last year's presidential campaign heated up, stories began circulating about how foreign banks, many with Russian connections, were financing his business ventures after his multiple bankruptcies. Both of his sons spoke of how much of their profits came from Russia. Other media outlets suggested that Russian bigshots had purchased apartments in New York City's Trump Towers as a money-laundering strategy. Others have highlighted how Mr. Trump's efforts to lend his name to luxurious housing in Moscow were put on hold in part because of United States government sanctions.

After Donald Trump became president, stories circulated about Russia's efforts to tamper with the campaign and of mysterious meetings in of-of-the-way places between representatives of the Trump administration and the Russian government to discuss ... well' no one knows. The day after the FBI director was fired, President Trump hosted two Russian government bigshots in the Oval Office, banning the United States press while giving the Russians supersecret information. More recently, we learned about that infamous meeting in June, 2016 in Trump Tower between Trump campaign leaders and Russian officials, followed by a sophisticated effort to hurt Hillary Clinton's campaign.

Investigations continue, along with inconvenient questions. To what extent, if any, did the Trump campaign collude with the dirty tricks of the Russian government? What does Vladimir Putin want in return? What materials might the Russians use to blackmail members of the Trump administration? Why won't Donald Trump release his tax returns?

So, Republicans, this is your chance to change the culture of the playground. You might start by asking yourselves if you would begin impeachment hearings if the name "Clinton" was substituted for "Trump." If the answer is "yes," will a group of you, like your forefathers did with President Nixon in 1974, forcefully but quietly tell President Trump that you no longer support his behavior, and unless he resigns, you will join Democrats' efforts to impeach him?

I suspect that, like most bullies, President Trump would back down from this show of force, but if he doesn't, stand strong. Ignore his tantrums. Point out to key influencers in the right wing ecosystem that chances to implement your policies will increase with a trustworthy president who will fight for them instead of a president who is incapable or unwilling to lead.

Many of us who disagree with your policies would appreciate your efforts to stop our ever-more-slippery slide into a muddy sandbox.

Perhaps, a few of the more moderate Democrats will support your efforts to repeal and replace Obamacare, reform the tax system, tackle our immigration problems, create and infrastructure program, destroy those radical Islamic terrorists, and give more control to the conservative Christian crowd.

Republicans, this is your big chance to shine. Don't blow it.

PART IX

CHRISTIANS AND CHRISTIANITY

Where I write about my faith journey; reflect on the dissonances between Christianity and disability; think about violence and forgiveness; meditate on Jesus' ministry; and ponder the meaning of peace.

THE POLITICS OF GOD IS LOVE

September 12, 2012

While celebrating my fifth anniversary with my wife, Lisa, at a peaceful setting in Hermann, Missouri, a corner of my brain was ruminating about how members of the Democratic convention had banned God from their platform. My first reaction was to dread the political fall-out. My second reaction was to note the futility of the act: God cannot be banned from anywhere unless He chooses to be. Then I remembered why I am a Christian who struggles with unbelief.

My dad was hostile towards Christianity because a Lutheran pastor had regularly hit him hard on the head with the bow of a cello because he couldn't sing in tune. He also resented the German Lutheran Church's support of Hitler during Hitler's rise to power.

My first connection with organized religion took place in high school when I was invited to sing in a folk group that played a part at the local Catholic church's noon mass. While I enjoyed the rehearsals, the priests' monotonous drone made it impossible for me to experience any sort of divine presence. My second high school experience with a church was far more positive, thanks to the dynamic and wise pastor who encouraged me to use my gifts to support others.

Saturday night partying and my circle of friends discouraged me from attending church services in college, and my feeble efforts to return to church after college were thwarted when ushers at one church wouldn't let me enter with my guide dog and ushers at another wanted me to sit alone in a balcony instead of among the congregation. I also treasured the chance to relax on Sundays after a hard week's work.

But Christian radio came to the rescue. At first, I snickered while preachers screeched about Godless communism, secular humanism, and how anyone can have anything they wanted if they prayed hard enough. These rantings became less funny as these preachers gained political power and after people started accosting me on the streets to tell me that I was blind because I didn't have enough faith.

But radio preachers caught my attention when they described how God influenced events through far-from-perfect kings, prophets, and disciples. Others had shown compassion and given sound psychological advice for people and families struggling with everyday challenges. Somehow, the salvation message seeped into my soul despite my irritation with preachers who railed against sexual sins at the expense of other misdeeds; demonized those who disagreed with them; and implied that sins of women and people without money were more harmful than those of men and people with money.

While working towards my social work degree, I was surprised by the agreements between secular and Christian counselors despite the contempt that both groups expressed towards each other. Most of my professors and many of my fellow students were vehemently hostile towards Christianity, contradicting the message drilled into us that we shouldn't judge.

Since moving to the midwest, I have joined the choir of the largest Methodist church in Columbia, Missouri. My oldest stepson attends meetings of a thriving youth group in another church.

But the most encouraging boost to my Christian faith has been Lisa's faith journey. Several weeks before we got married, she surprised me with her decision to commit to Christianity despite her prior complaints about the conniving, adulterous know-it-alls that she had met who bragged about their church attendance. She was baptized the day after our wedding.

As I write this, we are heading home from our anniversary get-away during which we visited a brewery and two wineries, ate too much good food, and spent time laughing, talking, remembering, cuddling, and praying together. Thanks, Lisa, for that beautiful prayer reflecting on the past and hoping for the future. Thanks for continuing to teach me how to love and forgive.

To those harumphing about the Democratic Party turning its back on

God, I encourage you to think about whether part of the problem is that we have been lousy ambassadors because of what we have and haven't said or done. To those who are irritated with God, I would urge you to consider the possibility that you are more angry at the actions of us Christians than at God. Nobody's perfect, and we might learn something if we pause long enough to listen soulfully to each other.

DRIVE-BY EVANGELISM

August 11, 2013

Several years ago, a woman greeted me in a cheery, elderly voice as Jules, my former guide dog, and I approached an intersection.

"Hi," I said, not interested in striking up a conversation.

"I have a dog, too," she chirped.

"I noticed," I said, hearing its panting as it tried to sniff Jules.

"She's a golden retriever," the woman explained, making no audible effort to control it.

"Oh," I mumbled, trying to keep Jules focused on me.

"Did you know that God restores sight to 4,679 blind people every day?" she asked.

"Um," I said, cringing inwardly. Many people who are blind and/or with other physical disabilities complain to anyone who will listen about complete strangers stopping us on the street to tell us that God will heal us if we have enough faith, or that we will go to hell unless we accept Jesus Christ as Lord and Savior.

"I read about it in a Russian magazine," she continued.

I was vaguely curious about the magazine's name, and how its reporter came up with that particular number.

"All you need is enough faith," she continued breathlessly.

I couldn't help wondering how many people God allows to become blind every day; after all, if He is all-powerful and always present—

Her voice quivered with excitement. "Would it be OK if I prayed for you?"

"Thanks," I said, trying not to be rude. I picked up Jules' harness and urged him forward. "But I'm in a hurry."

"God bless you," she called after us, "and remember that God restores sight to 4,679 blind people every day."

"God bless," I called over my shoulder, trying not to smirk.

For years, I thought that only people with physical disabilities had to face this irritation until I heard about pro-life prayer warriors shouting at women entering clinics where abortions are performed that they will go to hell if they murder their unborn babies.

Several years ago, I found myself leading a dialogue between employees who were gay and employees who called themselves Christians as part of a diversity training program for a large federal agency. The gay employees complained about receiving daily Bible quotes from their Christian colleagues. Towards the end of the discussion, I encouraged the Christian employees to stop sending the e-mails.

"But we have every right to do this," someone protested.

"Of course you do," I said. "But you've received plenty of feedback that these messages are making it more difficult for them to accept what you're trying to share."

(I also encouraged the employees who were gay to delete these messages and move on.)

So I ask those who feel compelled to invade the space of strangers to share the Gospel to remember that most people prefer loving behaviors over being pelted with Bible snippets. And when it feels right to share your Christian journey, give space for the Holy Spirit to do its work.

To all of us who have endured these drive-by evangelism experiences, let's do a better job of showing a bit more grace. Perhaps, if I had been a little more patient with that woman at the intersection, I could have asked to pray for her after she prayed for me. In my prayer, I might have asked for a more open mind, increased patience, and for God to show her that being blind, while often a major nuisance, is not the smothering obstacle she seemed to believe. Perhaps, we both could have learned something from this encounter or started some sort of relationship, but even if nothing had happened, grace lingers, often causing unexpected blessings.

INTO THE DITCH

February 14, 2017

"So, Peter," a former choir director asked from out of the blue towards the end of a rehearsal. "What do you think of the line 'Was blind, but now I see?'"

"Well," I gulped. "It's OK, I guess, but I prefer 'Was bound, but now I'm free.'"

Silence.

"After all, the hymn was written by someone in the slave trade," I continued. "And some African American churches use this line."

"But the line is clearly about spiritual blindness," a choir member called from across the room.

"True; but I wish some Christians would remember that."

And we all trooped into the sanctuary prepared to sing an arrangement of "Amazing Grace."

More than a year later, the church pastor preached about Jesus' contempt of the religious leaders of the time. I became distracted when she quoted Jesus' aphorism:

And if the blind lead the blind, both shall fall into the ditch. (Matthew 15, Verse 14, King James Version)

Another example of interpreting Scriptures through the lens of spiritual instead of physical blindness?

Well, we visually-impaired people don't usually lead each other into ditches.

Indeed, when we get together, we often walk in groups of up to ten people to restaurants, white canes tapping, guide dog tags jangling, with one or two leaders shouting directions to those behind us while those behind them call to the leaders to be sure they're not being left behind. We might look a bit weird to others, but then we find the Marco Polo game that light-dependent people play a bit silly. Regardless, we almost always get to where we want to go.

More recently, I came across the following quote from Jesus while reading Nadia Bolz-Weber's book *Accidental Saints:*

"When you give a banquet, invite the poor, the crippled, the lame, and the blind. And you will be blessed, because they cannot repay you, for you will be repaid at the resurrection of the righteous." (Luke, Chapter 14, Verses 13-14, New International Version)

In her book, Nadia Bolz-Weber argued that Jesus especially wants our uncool, lame, blind, poor, and crippled parts when we join Him at His table, and that while that vulnerability will make us uncomfortable, we will also feel some relief and be more at peace with ourselves and others.

A cool, even profound, bit of commentary.

Except that some of us blind folk are cool, and most of us can at least somewhat repay the community for the kindnesses that we receive from others if given the chance.

"Thanks for the offer," I regularly hear from church leaders when I offer to help with some sort of community outreach project. "We'll be in touch."

That's where the conversation usually ends.

So I'm less likely to reach out.

Spiritual blindness? Comforting, but vaguely condescending. If Jesus was all-knowing, why did He reinforce the stereotype that we people with visual impairments (and those with other disabilities) are poor, hopeless souls? What might He say differently if He roamed amongst us today?

I don't know, but I wish that each of us would reflect more on how our sometimes unconscious interpretations of Scripture reinforce stereotypes that make it more difficult for others to be more productive members of God's community.

FORGIVENESS COURAGE

November 25, 2014

I heard during a recent sermon about how a young African American woman saw her brother's dead body hanging from a tree late at night. Fear paralyzed her when she thought that she couldn't identify the assailants because they had covered their faces with sheets.

"But," the minister continued, "she began to gain the courage to forgive when it dawned on her that she could identify the assailants through the shoes they wore, as her job involved shining their shoes."

"How extraordinary," I thought, losing track of the sermon, "that she found the courage to forgive instead of the courage to avenge."

For forgiveness courage is much harder to get and to hold onto because most of us prize vengeance. Ideas such as "Don't get mad, get even!"; "Show them who's boss!"; and "Don't let them walk all over you!" ooze through our surroundings, and we often at least silently cheer when something bad happens to someone who we believe has done something wrong.

Avenging courage seems much easier to define. Someone does us wrong, and we find a way to make their life miserable, resulting in a short-term sense of accomplishment and cheers from our friends.

Faith communities encourage forgiveness, yet provide conflicting ideas concerning what it means. Must we forget those wrongs done to us? Must we maintain relationships with those who have hurt us as if the hurting never happened? To what extent are we allowed to protect ourselves from being harmed by those who have wronged us in the past?

I have been wrestling with the meaning of forgiveness since I started on my career path as customer service representative, grants manager, educator, human resources professional, and mediator. What does it mean to forgive the boss who forced me to resign because I did what she asked me to do? Or those bosses who took credit for my successes, blamed me for mistakes that others made, or didn't follow through on commitments? I find these behaviors especially hard to forgive because, as a person who is totally blind, it takes far more effort to land a job than my light-dependent peers.

When I expressed my frustration during a retreat several years ago, a participant provided me with a definition that has stuck with me ever since.

"Forgiveness," she told me, "is genuinely hoping that the person who's wronged you is moving in a good direction."

Forgiveness is both a journey and a choice. It doesn't mean forgetting the wrongs done or allowing the wrongdoer to injure me again without consequences. It requires patience, flexibility, and courage, for every situation is different.

So how well am I doing at forgiving those bosses who have put barriers in my way? I certainly haven't forgotten the damage they did to my career and self-confidence. I haven't made much of an effort to maintain contact with them. But over time, I have learned about how my impatience, stubbornness, and mistrust of authority made it harder for me to work well with people who project more confidence than they have.

Over the years, I've also learned that it's easier to forgive if I can be truly thankful of those bosses, family members, and dogs who have supported me in my quest to get better.

LET FREEDOM RING

July 2, 2015

Like most of us, I was humbled when a parade of family members of those that Dylann Roof murdered during the massacre at Emanuel African Methodist Episcopal (AME) Church forgave him during Mr. Roof's arraignment.

"You took something very precious from me, but I forgive you," said Nadine Collier, in between sobs. "It hurts me. You hurt a lot of people, but may God forgive you."

"If I had experienced something similar, I think I would have been too numb to even think about forgiving the murderer," I thought. "And why is it that African American churchgoers seem to be better at forgiving than us white churchgoers?"

"Because," I realized, "the average African American has more chances to understand the downside of not forgiving others and to practice the art of forgiveness. They have larger forgiveness muscles than the average white person."

Forgiveness takes courage. It takes grit. It takes perseverance, patience, and humility. It requires empathy, the ability to intuit how those different from us experience similar situations.

As I was pondering the mystery of forgiveness, a Fast Company article (1) caught my attention. It reported that salary raises and promotional opportunities diminished for women (and sometimes men) with female bosses when compared to those with bosses who are men.

This is disturbing to those of us who believe that salting organizations with talented women will lead to more women being promoted. Perhaps, organizations are doing a poor job of connecting women to their culture. Perhaps, workplace cultures are subtly discouraging women from promoting female peers. But I can't help wondering if the bitterness of women who have experienced the psychic scars borne from workplace discrimination influences the way they manage others. The only way to address this dynamic is for women (and members of other minority groups) to begin building up their forgiveness muscles while those with authority take concrete action to reduce the discrimination being experienced.

We might also remember that the best way to limit the size of government is to live together more peacefully, manage conflicts more soulfully, and to forgive each other more graciously. We could each start by reflecting on the meaning of that most famous hymn sung by President Obama during his eulogy of Clementa Pinckney, Emanuel AME Church's pastor:

"Amazing grace, how sweet the sound
That saved a wretch like me.
I once was lost, but now I'm found;
Was blind, but now I see."
Or, my preference for that last line:
"Was bound, but now I'm free."
Let freedom ring!

(1) https://www.fastcompany.com/3047826/strong-female-lead/why-isnt-having-more-women-in-leadership-budging-the-gender-wage-gap

JESUS THROUGH HARRY

May 14, 2016

"Each of us has an idea of who Jesus Christ is, what he was like, some of his personality traits and more," a colleague recently wrote to members of an on-line discussion list. "Would any of you care to share who Jesus is to you. What is his nature, and how does he express that to you?"

My first reaction was to run from the question. After all, Jesus is a mix of contradictions: god and man; and lamb and lion; to cite the most obvious. So how can one even answer such a question?

But remembering that many of us view Jesus through the lens of our biological fathers, I thought about how my dad was a wonderful teacher, storyteller, and advocate, but not particularly affectionate. Is that the way I view Jesus?

Maybe, but something's still missing.

Then, I thought about how J.K. Rowling wove Christian themes throughout the *Harry Potter* series. (1)

The Bible doesn't have much to say about Jesus' upbringing, and the *Harry Potter* series certainly isn't the Bible. But given the parallels between the two stories, I wonder if the Potter series offers some insights into Jesus' teenage years.

"Certainly not!" some conservative Christians might protest. "Harry lied. He got into fights. He broke rules. He disrespected authority figures. He was sarcastically angry. He needlessly led his friends into danger."

But was Jesus really the goody-two-shoes type while growing up? He certainly wasn't as an adult, according to the religious leaders of his time.

Like Jesus, Harry understood his unique mission: to destroy evil. But as Harry discovered through the series, people on the side of good are flawed, and people on the dark side have strengths.

This contradiction, combined with Harry's Christ-like nature and the clueless or cruel actions of authority figures around him, explains much of his wrongdoing. He lied and fought to protect his friends, including Ron and Ginny, from the Muggle-loving family; Hermione, the Mudblood; Neville, the fearful; Luna, the oddball; Lupin, the werewolf; Hagrid, the half-giant; and Dobby, the house-elf. With Hermione's assistance, he harnessed his sarcastic anger to training Dumbledore's Army for future battles.

While far from perfect, Harry was just a bit better than his peers. He thanked people and house-elves who helped him. He accepted the overly-harsh consequences of his rule-breaking without complaining too much. He quickly forgave Ron for his disloyalty in Book Four and desertion in Book Seven. He didn't gloat over his victories against Draco Malfoy, Professor Umbridge, and Lord Voldemort; indeed, he risked his life to save Draco's. His ability to read people was better than most, which made it possible for him to navigate through the morally ambiguous situations that appear throughout the series.

I wonder if, like Harry, Jesus developed into a leader of misfits while growing up. Or, being God, were these skills perfectly programed into Him so that all He had to do was to follow the path already laid out for him? Or does some middle ground exist? While I'm no theologian, instinct suggests that He couldn't be truly with us if He didn't have to walk along the sometimes difficult path of behavior change.

So who is Jesus to me?

A bundle of contradictions that understands, loves, and supports me so that I can change my bundle of contradictions to be more like His perfect nature.

Sometimes, He waits. Sometimes, He talks quietly. Sometimes, He shouts or does something more dramatic. Sometimes, I hear Him. Sometimes, I clearly understand Him, and less frequently, I follow His call.

Something's still missing, but that's OK, as meditation and time tend to make things more clear.

(1) http://www.mtv.com/news/1572107/harry-potter-author-jk-rowling-opens-up-about-books-christian-imagery/

KING WITH A HEART

March 23, 2016

During Pastor Kendall Walker's Palm Sunday sermon, he explained that both "King" Pilate, the Roman ruler of the area, and "King" Herod, the man who reported directly to Pilate, each preceded Jesus into Jerusalem, riding in chariots with large groups of noisy followers and battalions of soldiers for protection and an aura of strength. Like Pilate and Herod, King Jesus arrived in Jerusalem on a donkey — a Jewish symbol of royalty — with a large group of followers and showed his strength by cleansing the temple of unwelcomed merchants.

As the sermon continued, I thought about how, like in Jesus' day, interconnected bureaucracies of big business, big government, big military, and big religion seem to be getting more powerful at the expense of the rest of us. And that these big shots are lording it over us.

Yet the foundations on which these bumbling bureaucracies rest seem to be built on sand. They have nearly unlimited resources, but seem to be loosing control. Businessman Trump, Senators Sanders and Cruz, along with many others, are sending tremors through their foundations. Smaller, more agile businesses are siphoning away profits and prestige. After nearly fifteen years of continuous war, the military, despite its impressive array of high-tech killing machines, doesn't seem as omnipotent.

Later in his sermon, Pastor Kendall pointed out that Jesus' most harsh rhetoric was aimed at the rigid, corrupt, and soulless religious institutions of the day. Unlike Pilate, Herod, and the religious pooh-bahs of that time, Jesus divided his ministry between serving outcasts and preparing a motley crew of disciples to continue His ministry. He miraculously healed the sick and fed the hungry. He comforted the down-hearted. He talked about the power of meekness, righteousness, mourning, forgiveness, and peacemaking, often telling stories to clarify His countercultural concepts.

Today, many leaders within these lumbering interconnected bureaucracies use Jesus' techniques to build skills among those they lead. They model the behaviors they want. They tell stories to reinforce concepts. They nurture their followers and break down barriers to make success more likely.

So what about these behemoths cause them to be so ineptly powerful? Or powerfully inept?

Bill Walton, a hall-of-fame basketball player, provided an answer.

During an interview on ESPN Radio, one of the hosts asked him about his relationship with John Wooden, the clean-cut, venerated UCLA men's basketball coach during the 1970's, and Jerry Garcia, the venerated leader of the countercultural band The Grateful Dead. Bill spoke about how both men were far more interested in making their followers the best they could be than indulging in life's luxuries. He spoke about how, after butting heads with Coach Wooden about hair length, clothes, and politics, he always did what the coach asked.

"Because," he said, "all of us knew that Coach Wooden had our best interests at heart."

"That's it!" I thought. "Jesus, through his actions, character, and charisma, communicated to his followers that He had their best interests at heart, even when He said things that were hard to hear or understand. And the leadership of behemoth bureaucracies, through their actions, character, and charisma, convey that, ultimately, it's all about the bureaucracy."

Most of Jesus' followers deserted him before the authorities tortured and crucified Him, perhaps because of a mixture of fear and a sense of betrayal. "We thought you were going to help us get rid of these creeps, but you're allowing them to kill you; what's up with that?"

A blessed Good Friday.

But everything soon changed.

Happy Easter!

THE ANTICHRIST PARLOR GAME

December 20, 2016

Since at least 1980, Christian end of the world experts have claimed on mainstream conservative Christian outlets that each United States president was the antichrist, the demon with some connection with the number 666, who will unite, then trash, the world until Jesus Christ's glorious return. Jimmy Carter, because he helped negotiate a peace treaty between Israel and Egypt. Ronald Wilson Reagan, because each of his names contains six letters. George H. W. Bush, because of his one-world-order pronouncements. Bill Clinton, because of his commitment to the one world order and his sexual exploits in the Oval Office. George W. Bush, because, well, he's a Bush. Barack Hussein Obama, because he isn't a US citizen but is a Muslim committed to the one world order and might become the next head of the United Nations, the epitome of corrupt evildoing one-world-orderdom.

About a month before Donald Trump was promoted from bully businessman/entertainer to President-Elect, I suggested, tongue firmly in cheek, in an e-mail to a conservative Christian discussion group that he might be the antichrist because of his charisma and close alliance with Russia's strong man Vladimir Putin.

"Nonsense," I was told. "President Obama has more charisma than Donald Trump, and in any case, the Bible indicates that the antichrist is either homosexual or not interested in sex."

Why prior end time experts didn't include this nugget is beyond me, but I see clearly now that Donald Trump can't be the antichrist due to his welcomed and unwelcomed sexual conquests.

Might he be the new Messiah, however?

Yes.

According to Brian Tashman's (1) article on Right Wing Watch, end times pastor Tom Horn stated that Donald Trump might be the messiah or his forerunner, and that the antichrist will become visible soon.

Praise the Lord!

But I have a different theory.

Perhaps, strong man Putin is the antichrist with Donald Trump serving as his willing or unwilling assistant.

According to end time experts, the antichrist is supposed to be a power-hungry deceiver from Europe. Mr. Putin, formerly of the KGB, became Russia's Mr. Christian Revivalist until recently, when he has forbidden evangelical Christians from spreading the good news within Russia. Yet he still is anti-gay rights, anti-abortion rights, and in favor of killing as many Muslims as possible, beliefs that most United States conservative Christians share. He seems to have played a small but significant role in President-Elect Trump's promotion.

There's more.

According to those Christian radio end time experts, conditions have never been aligned so closely with end time conditions. Russia and Iran on the same side for the first time ever. Global warming and earthquakes in strange places. Israel increasingly threatened. Ever-more-powerful computers.

How does the United States fit into this?

The Bible doesn't say, but suppose President-Elect Trump abandons Israel in favor of a strong alliance with President Putin's Russia. Then, according to Bible prophecies, both the United States and Russia would be destroyed when God saves Israel from its enemies, thus removing both nations as players in future end time events.

Do I believe this?

No. The Bible counsels us not to try to predict what will happen when, and end time experts disagree about what Bible prophecies foretell. It seems unlikely that the Trump administration would abandon Israel.

But I think my end time theory is more likely than the all-United-States-presidents-are-antichrists, or the Donald-Trump-is-the-Messiah pronouncements. And it would be ironic if those who are so certain about the rightness of their beliefs would be the first to be deceived.

I do believe, though, that it's the end of the world as we know it. And I don't feel fine.

(1) http://www.rightwingwatch.org/post/end-times-pastor-donald-trump-could-be-the-messiah-or-his-forerunner/

CURTAINS AND MUSLINS

June 18, 2017

In a dark, musty cave on top of an Alaskan snow-swept mountain, seven Curtain men knelt to pray.

"Brothers," Sampson said in an urgent voice after prayers ended. "We have suffered for far too long. It's time to begin to reclaim our former glory."

"Amen," chorused the rest of the group.

The descent into ignominy was achingly familiar. The shooting of that martyred Congressman Steve Scalise fifty years earlier was the start of the second United States Civil War. Red Curtains vs. blue Curtains. Massive mayhem. Death, torture, plagues, and starvation. Heroism and cowardice. The red Curtains gloriously victorious.

But in the massive celebrations, the Muslins, with assistance from that Curtain traitor Vladimir Putin, conquered the United States.

"But what can we do?" Joshua asked bitterly. "The Muslins control everything. They have bribed those blue Curtains that still remain to continue the Civil War. We have few weapons, and those Muslin defenses are impenetrable."

"Faith, brother!" counseled Elijah. "We can't afford to feel sorry for ourselves. Besides, all is not lost."

"That's right," Sampson interrupted. "We have supporters scattered about. And we still have a couple of star-smashers."

"Praise the Lord!" several men shouted.

"Hush," counseled Gideon. "The wind has ears."

"Star what?" asked Isaiah.

"You know," Joshua said impatiently. "A weapon that smashes every creature in its path 700 miles in every direction from its detonation point."

"Muslin defenses are almost impregnable," warned Samuel.

"And the longer we wait, the more impregnable the Muslin defenses will become!" snapped Joshua.

"There's a time for everything under heaven," boomed Elijah. "And I say it's time to kill! Destroy! And out of the fire will come a new heaven and earth."

"Praise the Lord!" six men shouted, their voices louder than before.

"Hold on!" a quiet voice cut through the din.

"Yes, brother?" Elijah asked.

"Brothers," Isaiah said in a calm, soothing voice. "Surely you remember how we controlled those Muslins those many years ago."

An uneasy pause.

"Of course we did our share of killing radical Muslin terrorists," Isaiah continued. "But beginning under that consummate Curtain Ronald Reagan, we sold weapons to Muslins of all persuasions and cheered silently as they killed each other."

"Those were glorious days," Elijah said reverently.

"So the tables have turned!" interrupted Gideon. "It's time to use the Muslin strategies against them!"

"Praise the Lord!" bounced off cave walls.

"Brothers," Isaiah pleaded.

Shouts subsided into surly silence.

"Is that what we're put here for?" Isaiah asked. "Kill or be killed forever and ever?"

An ominous silence.

"What about peace-making? Long-suffering? Loving our enemies?"

"We've heard this before from you," mumbled Elijah.

"Be silent, brother Isaiah!" rasped Gideon.

"What about nonviolence?" Isaiah continued. "Gandhi? King?"

"Apostates!" shouted Sampson.

"Toss him out!" Joshua bellowed.

"Traitor!" several others yelled.

"And what about the research that shows that nonviolent actions are twice as likely to succeed than violence?" Isaiah pleaded.

"Science!" scoffed Elijah.

"Sampson, would you do the honors?" Joshua asked.

"Yes, brother!" Sampson said, silencing Isaiah with one punch. Isaiah's mouth moved in silent prayer as Sampson threw him over his shoulder and hurried outside.

"Gideon, would you draw up a plan of action?" Joshua asked.

"It would be an honor, brother."

"We'll pray for you," Sampson told Isaiah, his voice barely carrying over the wind-driven snow. Isaiah's lips continued to move in prayer as Sampson threw him off a seventy-foot cliff.

Sampson returned to the relative warmth of the cave as Gideon began to plan the attack.

"We need to pray!" he interrupted.

PEACE

December 22, 2014

"Glory to God in the highest," the angels sang as they announced the birth of Jesus to the shepherds. "And peace to his people on earth."

Over the years, I have heard many sermons about the Christmas story, but I don't recall coming across any reflections on the meaning of peace.

So...what is peace?

A perusal of the on-line Free Merriam-Webster Dictionary and the Oxford (American English) dictionary yields the following definition:

Freedom from disquieting or oppressive thoughts or emotions; freedom from, or the cessation of, war or violence; freedom from dispute or dissension between individuals or groups.

Since "disquieting or oppressive thoughts or emotions", war, violence, and "dispute or dissension between individuals or groups" are examples of conflict, peace can be defined as freedom from, or cessation of, conflict.

But can we really be free of conflict?

In what circumstances are you most likely to feel most at peace?

For me, it's sitting alone in a comfortable chair on the deck of my house. Birds are calling to each other. A cooling breeze is whistling through the leaves. The sun is warm, but not hot. A dog is barking from somewhere down the street.

Or I'm relaxing with people who I love.

Or I'm listening to an inspiring piece of music.

Each of these instances are examples of peace-inducing environments, but are they conflict-free?

Birds call to each other to mark their territory or to seek out sex partners. The breeze and the sun increase the evaporation of water which, if not replaced, will, over time, result in a dessert-like environment. The leaves the breeze are rustling will soon die to make way for new ones in the spring. The trees that house the leaves crowd out other vegetation or flowers.

In order to relax around people I love, we must be able to feel safe around each other, which requires constant positive communication and other trust-building behaviors. That relaxing and inspiring music would not be possible without painstaking work of those that composed and performed it.

So those relaxants hum with conflict as living things cooperate and compete with each other to thrive. When conditions get too out of sync, watch out!

The same is true for us. Conflict is an ever-present companion, whether at home, on the job — anywhere we go. Conflicts can be small or big, and take place between people, among groups, and within ourselves. If not properly managed, watch out!

So how do we manage conflicts, as they usually can't be fully resolved?

Sometimes, we work towards improving relationships, either with others or ourselves. Sometimes, we look for help from others. Sometimes, we negotiate. Sometimes, we change our behavior to prevent a conflict from starting or getting worse. Sometimes, we walk away, hoping that a better chance will come to address the conflict or that it will manage itself. Sometimes, we decide to let the other win. Sometimes, we fight, using any weapon within reach.

Each of these peace-building strategies can be effective, depending on our strengths, personalities, and the situation. But we will defeat ourselves if we don't recognize that peace is not the freedom from conflict, but conflict well managed.

God promises to be there for His people to support our peace-building efforts.

Merry Christmas!

Printed in the United States
By Bookmasters